It's easy to define forgiveness  it's not really possible to do i
find its healing power. Craig S ___ ___ ___ the
same tattered platitudes we've heard before. This is a
fresh look behind the scenes of grief, injustice, and the
miracle of forgiveness.

—MARK RUTLAND
BEST-SELLING AUTHOR AND FOUNDER OF THE NATIONAL
INSTITUTE OF CHRISTIAN LEADERSHIP

After a head-on collision took the lives of his loved
ones, my dear friend Craig Stone in his book *Forgiving the Unforgivable* takes on the subject of anger,
depression, and forgiveness head-on! This riveting
true story of tragedy, anger, healing, and forgiveness
has the power to break through major roadblocks for
others to receive and give forgiveness. Powerful and a
must-read!

—JIM BOLIN
SENIOR PASTOR, TRINITY CHAPEL
POWDER SPRINGS, GEORGIA

I have known Craig Stone for many years. Around
twenty years ago a horrific car accident resulted in
the deaths of three of Craig's family members. Sadly
the driver was never punished. He simply went free
after a lengthy trial. Craig could have let bitterness
destroy him. But praise be to God that did not happen.
Craig was able to forgive the driver, and in doing so
he saved himself from the effects of bitterness on his
own body and health.

Let me explain what I mean by that. Human beings
have been given a "fight or flight response" by God.
This means that when we are in danger, we either

fight or run away. The problem is that when we are under extreme, long-term stress or bitterness, we can't always run. We have to continually deal with the situation with no means of escape. Over time our bodies pay a heavy price. The risks of cancer, arthritis, heart disease, and diabetes all go through the roof. This continual stress causes decreased digestion, which causes poor nutrient absorption, which causes disease and accelerated aging.

That is why you have to read this book. It is a book of learning how to forgive and thereby learning how to live stress-free God's way. Your health and the health of your family members may depend on you putting into practice the principles that Craig Stone teaches us. This book may literally save your life!

—Ted Broer
International best-selling author
Founder of Health Masters
www.healthmasters.com

Craig Stone is truly an anointed man of God who loves the Lord with all of his heart. He is a powerful minister with an amazing gift to bring healing to hurting, broken people. His message reaches out to people who have gone through a tragedy in their life. His book was birthed out of his own personal tragedy when three of his family members were killed in a car accident. As you read this book, you can feel and even relate to his pain. You catch a glimpse of Craig's inner struggle and how he battled to hold on to his faith in a time of great darkness. Craig opens his life up to you as he honestly talks of how the devil tried to manipulate him into an act of revenge. He even confesses his desire to harm the person driving the car that killed his family. This book is filled with the amazing grace of God's healing power, and Craig tells how the Lord helped him to overcome his anger, his hatred, and his bitterness. And after all the injustice he went through, God gave Craig the power to forgive.

If you've ever had anyone to hurt you or if you've ever been through a tragedy, you need to read this book. It will heal your heart and enable you to release your hatred and give you the grace to forgive your trespasser. This book is filled with inner healing for bruised and broken hearts.

—JEFF PREWER
PASTOR, FREEDOM LIFE CHURCH OF GOD
HENDERSON, NORTH CAROLINA

FORGIVING THE
UNFORGIVABLE

CRAIG STONE

CHARISMA
HOUSE

Most CHARISMA HOUSE BOOK GROUP products are available at special quantity discounts for bulk purchase for sales promotions, premiums, fund-raising, and educational needs. For details, write Charisma House Book Group, 600 Rinehart Road, Lake Mary, Florida 32746, or telephone (407) 333-0600.

FORGIVING THE UNFORGIVABLE by Craig Stone
Published by Charisma House
Charisma Media/Charisma House Book Group
600 Rinehart Road
Lake Mary, Florida 32746
www.charismahouse.com

Cover design by Lisa Rae McClure
Design Director: Justin Evans

Visit the author's website at www.craigstone.org.

Library of Congress Cataloging-in-Publication Data:
Stone, Craig.
  Forgiving the unforgivable / by Craig Stone. -- First
edition.
      pages cm
  Includes bibliographical references.
  ISBN 978-1-62136-986-8 (trade paper) -- ISBN 978-1-
62136-987-5 (e-book)
  1. Forgiveness--Religious aspects--Christianity. 2. Grief-
-Religious aspects--Christianity. I. Title.
  BV4647.F55S745 2015
  234'.5--dc23

                                              2014045990

Names related to those involved in the accident and
subsequent trial have been changed.

15 16 17 18 19 — 98765432
Printed in the United States of America

In memory of my father, Rev. Fred Carold Stone; my grandmother Pauline Hunt; and my great-grandmother Retha Williams

CONTENTS

ACKNOWLEDGMENTS

To Janet, my wife and best friend—thank you for your support, your love, and your companionship. You are truly a gift from God.

To Matthew, Valerie, and Jonathan, my children—words can never express how much I love you. I am so proud of you.

To Diana Stone and Adrienne Gaines, my editors—thank you for your commitment, guidance, faith, and stamina throughout this project.

To David, my brother—thank you for your support throughout this journey.

Finally to my mother, Judith Stone—thank you for always believing in me and for praying that I would make a difference in this world for the kingdom of God. Your love and support have been priceless.

FOREWORD

SPEND A WEEK watching the news or reading the newspaper, and you will find people who have many reasons to be angry and unforgiving toward those who have harmed them. Throughout our lives we are guaranteed to encounter people who will mistreat us, offend us, or commit evil acts against us. There is no way around it.

If we aren't careful, we will allow those experiences to cause bitterness and unforgiveness to take root in our hearts. Harboring bitterness, unforgiveness, and a desire for revenge harms us physically, relationally, and spiritually; it does not settle any scores.

What keeps us from forgiving those who have offended or harmed us? Sometimes our pride, stubbornness, or fear of appearing weak will keep us bound in anger and unforgiveness. Other times our demand for justice keeps us from obeying God's command that we forgive others. Whatever our excuse, we cannot deny that the Bible tells us we must forgive.

Craig Stone and I are first cousins, and I still remember the moment I heard the news of the accident that killed three of his relatives. The enemy was out to destroy Craig's life. Indeed, at times I was afraid Craig would have a mental breakdown over this tragedy. When we allow rage and unforgiveness to become strongholds in our lives, those sins also become roadblocks that cut off our peace and joy. It was a long road to recovery, but by the grace of God, Craig made it through the ordeal.

I have seen the Lord use Craig's story to help other people who have lost family members through tragic circumstances, especially those whose loved ones were killed in drunk-driving accidents. There is no question that God uses our own trials and adversities to help other people who are experiencing similar struggles.

If you are dealing with circumstances that have caused you to live with bitterness and unforgiveness, I believe you will be blessed by this book. God is our anchor and His Word is our truth. If we allow ourselves to be changed by the power of God and the truth of His Word, we will overcome. God can then use our adversity to help others overcome.

In this book Craig tells his personal story of the events leading up to and following the accident that claimed the lives of several of his family members. Then he delves into a study of grief and forgiveness. Through Craig's story you will learn that, while we cannot deny or avoid the pain that other people create in our lives, through the grace of God we can learn to face it, overcome it, forgive the offender, and find healing.

—JENTEZEN FRANKLIN
SENIOR PASTOR, FREE CHAPEL
AUTHOR OF *New York Times* BEST SELLER *Fasting*

FOREWORD

THE FIRST TIME I met Craig Stone and his family was during a revival in West Virginia. I stayed in the home of his parents when I was eighteen years old, and right away I could tell that they were a strong Christian family with unwavering faith in Christ. When I heard about the accident that killed his dad and other family members, I was stunned.

My own dad had a dream, just weeks before the accident, about a terrible wreck on the same road. Dad said, "This was a terrible accident, Perry. A car was hit by a drunk driver, and people were killed." When the Lord showed my dad something in a dream, we took it seriously. Dad warned me about the dream, because he knew that I was driving back and forth along that road during a revival.

After the accident and the trial that followed, I wondered how Craig would be able to forgive the driver. I was certain I would have struggled with unforgiveness had I been in his shoes.

It might be impossible to find a person who has not suffered hurts and wounds that were caused by someone who allowed the enemy to control their actions or even their tongue. People can be cruel and heartless sometimes. They do and say things that have the ability to pierce us like a fiery arrow and burn into our soul, sometimes affecting us for years. There is only one way to dislodge those arrows, and that is through a procedure called forgiveness.

Forgiveness is not a natural response, and it does not come easily. I have met people who have suffered terribly at the hands of others, and sometimes it takes awhile to work through a process that leads to forgiveness.

When we allow God to help us forgive someone who harmed us, or when we are forgiven by someone we have harmed, wounds are healed, relationships are restored, and we are brought back into fellowship with God. The entire Christian agenda revolves around forgiveness and love.

We never know how we will react to wounds caused by others until we are faced with a terrible situation. But the fact remains that God does not want us to live with unresolved anger, rage, and unforgiveness. He wants us to follow the words and example of Jesus and forgive those who have done nothing to deserve our forgiveness.

If you are bound by a stronghold of unforgiveness, let this book show you how to untangle yourself through obedience to God's Word. If you have been pierced by the enemy's arrows, you can dislodge them by practicing forgiveness. Don't continue to carry something that God wants you to place at His feet. Obey God and forgive. Allow Him to bring healing to your life.

—PERRY STONE
FOUNDER AND PRESIDENT,
VOICE OF EVANGELISM OUTREACH MINISTRIES

Chapter 1

A FATEFUL NIGHT

HAS THE JURY reached a verdict?"

"We have, your honor."

It was April 1993. Three hours and twenty minutes after beginning deliberations, the jury returned to the packed courtroom to issue their verdict. The case had been stacked against us; we knew it months before the trial began. But the final decision lay not with the attorneys, the judge, or the witnesses who would frequently twist the truth or commit outright perjury. The final outcome rested with twelve people—in this case, eight men and four women.

"How finds the jury?"

"On the charge of criminally negligent homicide, three counts, we the jury find the defendant: not guilty."

That verdict would crush our family and profoundly affect many of us for years to come. Even today some of our relatives remain locked in heartache and unforgiveness over the tragic events of that fateful night when our family members were killed in a car accident and by the injustice later committed in the courtroom.

For years after the verdict I was consumed with grief and had more than my share of anger—not just because of the loss but because of the trial that followed. We had sought only one thing: justice. But how is that possible when a legal system that prides itself on fairness seems to reward criminal behavior? If there is no fairness or justice, revenge is the next best thing, right?

Twenty years ago I was—and today by the grace of God still am—a minister of the gospel. That makes this confession even more difficult. I confess that I wanted revenge. I confess that I was so full of rage I wanted to kill the other driver involved in the accident that killed my family.

Grief is a natural and therefore predictable reaction to loss. But unresolved anger that kindles a flame of bitterness and unforgiveness is not only unhealthy, but it is also unbiblical. Peeling away the layers of pain to deal with the sin of bitterness and unforgiveness is not easy for most people, and by no means does it come naturally. I know this firsthand.

But I also know the freedom that comes when we release that anger and bitterness by choosing to forgive. I'm not talking about lip service—I'm talking about the kind of forgiveness that no longer keeps score and no longer seeks revenge, a forgiveness that frees us once and for all from the hurt and pain and leaves us with peace, joy, and hope for the future.

In the pages of this book I will show how God restored my hope and how He can do the same for you. Whether you've been divorced; lost a loved one, a business, or a job; been abused or betrayed; by God's grace it is possible to forgive even those things we think are unforgivable. It is possible to have a life of joy and freedom even after we've been dealt a devastating blow.

God is able to destroy the traumatic effects of the unexpected attacks on our lives. He is for us, not against us. I know that now, and twenty years after my life was turned upside down, I am finally able to tell the story.

• • • • • • •

My destiny was to become an evangelist and preach the gospel, and that is what I had been doing the night our family's lives changed forever. I was preaching at a church in Alexandria, Virginia. At the same time, evangelist Perry Stone, a long-time friend who claims me as a distant cousin though we have no genealogical proof, was preaching a revival at a church in a neighboring state. That revival had continued longer than expected, but Perry stayed until he could no longer postpone his next revival. He told the pastor that he must close the meeting on Friday night so he could travel to the next church.

Our revival in Alexandria ended the same time. I was driving back home when the pastor of the church called me. "We've been having a great revival and I don't want to end it yet," he said. "Can you come to our church and fill in for Perry?"

"Sure," I replied. "I have company coming to town next week, but I have some time open, so I'll be glad to come and preach."

We were expecting several of our family members to come: my parents, Fred and Judith Stone; my maternal grandmother, Pauline Hunt, and her husband, Richard; and my maternal great-grandmother, Retha Williams. Dad was a pastor who was then serving at a church in Benson, North Carolina. He was my hero and a perfect role model. An honorable and loving man, he always believed in me and was quick to let me know he was proud of my accomplishments. Ours was a treasured relationship, and I had great respect for him. Even as a teenager, I bit my tongue if ever I was tempted to say something disrespectful to him. He was the kind of man that any son would be proud to call Dad.

His middle name was Carold—Fred Carold Stone— and he had an identical twin brother named Harold. While my parents had only two children—my brother, David, and me—Dad had so many brothers and sisters that it was hard to keep track of all twenty-six of them. Dad's mother birthed eighteen children before she died at age thirty-nine. Later his dad remarried, and they had eight more children.

Tall and stately, Dad was an intelligent man who once had been a teacher and had even taught math and calculus to some of his own siblings in school. He had served as a school principal, a mathematician, and a certified public accountant. He was successful in life, but he remained a humble man who always considered other people over himself.

Pastoring churches came later in life. Dad could do just about anything except sing. I am a singer as well as a minister, and when I conducted revivals at Dad's church, I always told the sound manager, "If Dad starts to sing along with me, please turn down his microphone." He didn't get the gift to carry a tune, but he didn't care. He sang anyway because he loved the Lord and enjoyed life.

I was the first grandchild, and my grandmother Pauline was always special, almost like a mother to me. My great-grandmother Retha was Pauline's mother and my own mom's grandmother. As a young child, I could not understand why I had two grandmothers, so I referred to my great-grandmother Retha as "Two-Mom." The name stuck, so from then on, her nickname was Two-Mom.

This is the family who would be traveling to visit us on Tuesday, and all of us were looking forward to the visit. Our children were close to their grandparents, and their grandparents loved them in return, as do all good grandparents.

Their visit would be short because Dad planned to leave on Saturday and return to his own church for services on Sunday. My desire was to spend that limited time with my family instead of continuing the revival. But I preached two services at the church, and the revival spirit was strong. The pastor wanted me to stay, so I agreed, rather reluctantly, to continue the revival through Wednesday night.

"I'M GOING TO HEAR MY SON PREACH!"

On Tuesday, April 28, 1992, Dad and the other family members left North Carolina and started on the trip. Along the way they had car trouble. The trip that was expected to take eight hours took so long that they did not arrive at our home until two o'clock on the morning of Wednesday, April 29.

By then they were exhausted. Dad, being the easygoing guy who never complained, said, "You don't have any extra room, so I'll sleep right here on the floor." He placed a pillow on the floor and fell asleep. When he awoke several hours later, he left to visit his sister and other relatives.

Later that day Dad returned from visiting family, and he played with our children. Matthew, our oldest child, was ten at the time; our daughter, Valerie, was eight; and our youngest son, Jonathan, was six.

The three of them were having such a good time with Dad that I suggested they stay home instead of going to church that night. "You got in late, and you must be tired. Why don't you stay here and spend time with the kids? I can go to church tonight, or Janet can go with me, and I'll preach and close the meeting. We'll have Thursday and Friday together before you leave to go back home. We'll spend a couple of days having fun with the family."

But they wouldn't hear of it. Dad said, "No, no, I'm going to hear my son preach!"

My grandmother Pauline chimed in, "I haven't heard my grandson preach, and I'm going." She was determined to make that one-hour trip to church to hear her firstborn grandson preach.

Twelve of us headed to the revival that night. We piled into two cars and drove down the interstate. My wife, Janet, our children Jonathan and Valerie, Janet's friend Maria, and one of her children rode in the car that I drove, while the entire family from North Carolina and our son Matt rode with Dad. Five generations were with us that night, from our children Matthew, Jonathan, and Valerie, to their great-great grandmother Retha.

About an hour after we left home, we arrived at the church. The family chose their seats, and I took my seat at the front. The pastor opened the service, and we knew right away from the Holy Spirit's presence that this was going to be a powerfully anointed service. The pastor introduced me, and I took my place at the podium to preach the last sermon of the revival.

As I was standing on the platform, my eyes scanned the crowd and stopped briefly on my family. I thought, "What a wonderful sight to see my family—five generations—sitting together on one pew."

The service was outstanding that night. As I preached, I noticed that Dad would stand up occasionally, which indicated to me that he was enjoying the service. It was as though he wanted me to know that he was cheering me on. Later Janet told me that Dad nudged her throughout the service and said, "Boy, he's preaching good."

We concluded the service by asking those who wanted prayer to come forward. The altar quickly filled with people, including my grandmother Pauline.

An elegant and beautiful woman, she had developed a growth on her neck that she planned to have checked when she returned home. That night we prayed for the Lord to heal her.

I wanted to call Dad forward to help us pray for people, but I could not see him anywhere in the congregation. My eyes searched throughout the church until I finally spotted him all alone in the far distant corner, dancing in the Spirit. In all my life I had never seen Dad do that.

After we prayed for each person and the service ended, we decided to go somewhere to eat. Since Shoney's was one of the few places open that late, all twelve of us, along with the pastor and several church members, stopped there to enjoy a meal and fellowship. About twenty people were together at the restaurant that night. As we entered the restaurant, I told Dad, "Tonight the meal is on me. You get anything you want to eat."

"I believe I will," he said. Dad was six foot two, thin, and could eat whatever he wanted and never gain weight. And that night he ate everything he wanted, including dessert.

It was getting late, and the children had to attend school the next day. So once we had finished eating, we reluctantly parted from the church family, paid the bill, and headed to the parking lot. Matt asked if he could ride with his granddad, and we agreed to let him.

When leaving the Shoney's parking lot, there are two different routes that take you back home. You either turn right to drive back via the interstate or turn left to travel a shortcut down a two-lane road. Since it was already 11:30 p.m., I decided to take the faster route. I told Dad, "I know a shortcut; follow me."

"All right," he said.

The passengers loaded into the cars. I pulled out of the parking lot and turned left, while Dad followed closely behind me.

It had started to rain a light mist. We were traveling a two-lane road that was considered dangerous among local residents because there were unsafe curves in a few locations. Impatient drivers tended to illegally pass slower traffic on a double line, and some parts of the road had narrow shoulders with ditches. Along some sections of the roadway there was nowhere to go except into the ditch if an irresponsible driver was racing toward you in your own lane.

Local drivers knew it was important to be alert and cautious when driving this road. Adding to the problem, some areas were not well lit at night, and now it was misting rain. But we would be traveling through a rural area, and there was no reason for most people to be on this road at midnight in the middle of the week. We should encounter little traffic because by this time of night most people were home asleep. In less than an hour we should be home.

Chapter 2

FOREVER CHANGED

JANET WAS IN the front passenger seat of our car, and Jonathan was between the two of us. Maria and the other children were seated in the back. As I drove, Janet, Maria, and I were talking about the revival and enjoying our conversation.

About forty-five minutes had passed, and we were about a mile outside our city limits. I knew that I was coming upon one of the unsafe curves on the road. Almost as soon as the thought entered my mind, I saw headlights coming directly toward us. Instead of cautiously staying in his own lane, the driver was headed directly into the path of oncoming traffic—and that oncoming traffic happened to be our car!

I yelled, "Janet! That car's coming right at us! It's going to hit us!" Instinctively I threw my right hand out to protect Jonathan while simultaneously shouting, "Jesus!" I turned the steering wheel quickly to the right, even though I knew there was a ditch on the side of the road. Thankfully that move caused the oncoming car to hit only the front end of the driver's side of our car instead of slamming into us head-on. The impact immediately ruptured my left front tire, causing it to explode.

From that point on, everything seemed to happen in slow motion. It felt as though our car was floating across the field, though we were actually in the ditch. We were still moving on three tires and one rim, and our car was headed straight toward a utility pole. My foot was heavy on the brake as I cried out, "Jesus! Jesus! Jesus!"

Suddenly it felt as though somebody slowed down the car, and we barely bumped the utility pole. We were all shocked and still wondering what had just happened.

I looked around the car and asked, "Is everybody OK?" All appeared to be fine, but now we were in the ditch and not sure how to get out of the car.

Still stunned, Janet said, "Something's wrong."

"We're OK," I assured her. "We're OK!"

But she insisted, "I have to get out of this car. Something has happened." She didn't know what happened; she just knew *something* had happened.

Janet moved to open her passenger door, but I begged her not to get out. "It's too dark outside and it's misting rain, and we're here on this bad road. You could get out there and get hit by a car."

But Janet was determined to get out of the car. After several attempts she was able to open her door and step out into the ditch. She made her way quickly down the road behind our car, and that is when she came upon the accident.

After hitting us, the driver of the other car had continued driving on the wrong side of the road and hit the car behind us head-on at full speed. Even in the darkness and misty rain Janet could see that the car had been split in half from front to back. The car on the wrong side of the road had slammed the other car into a field beside the highway about twenty-five yards from our car. Smoke was rising from the wrecked vehicle; Janet feared it would burst into flames, but she didn't run from the car because when she got close enough she heard moaning.

The rest of us were still trying to help one another out of the car and then out of the ditch. We took time to make certain nobody was injured. Still unaware of the second accident, I told the group, "I'm going to flag down Dad's car and let him know we're OK."

Since Janet had run ahead of us, I yelled, "Janet!", as I ran in the direction she had gone. When I reached the place where Janet stood, my heart sank. This was Dad's car! This was my family!

THE MOST HORRIFIC SIGHT

If you can imagine seeing an accident on television or on a road you're traveling, multiply the shock and horror by a thousand times. That's how it feels when it is your own family. My parents were in the front seat, and my son Matt was somewhere in that car. We didn't know whether he was in the front seat or the back, because we did not see him get into the car when we left the restaurant. We looked, but he was nowhere to be found.

Dad was in the driver's seat, badly injured and barely conscious. He was saying, "Get it off me! Please get it off me!" He was trying to turn the key in the ignition. The impact had injured him so badly that apparently he thought something was crushing his body. There was also a bleeding wound that started at his forehead and continued across the top of his head. I knew he was in terrible condition, but I did not want to believe it was as serious as it appeared.

His eyes were on me, but I could tell he was in unbearable pain. Later we learned that the impact had broken nearly every bone in his body. Everything in my being wanted to remain positive, so I assured him, "Dad! Hang in there! Everything's going to be OK!"

Dad's only response was, "Get it off me." He still tried to turn the key in the ignition, but I'm sure he was in so much pain and shock that he had no idea what he was doing. Still reassuring him, I said, "Just hang in there, Dad! We'll get help out here. Everything's going to be OK!"

My grandmother Pauline was bent over in the back-seat and appeared to be unconscious. Her husband, Richard, was conscious, but his face was bleeding profusely. My great-grandmother Retha was also unconscious.

My mother was in the front passenger seat, injured and moaning, and all the while saying, "Get him off my legs." We didn't know what she was referring to because we could not get the jammed car door open. Meanwhile, Janet's friend Maria was standing on the other side of the road with the children, and now Valerie and Jonathan were crying.

Still in a controlled panic, Janet and I tried with all our strength to open the front passenger door as Mom kept moaning, "He's on my leg." We were able to pry open the door just enough to see that Matt was on the floorboard, pressed between the crushed car and Mom's legs. Somehow we managed to open the door far enough to pull him out. He appeared to be badly injured and unconscious, so we carefully wrapped him in something and placed him on the ground.

We later learned that we should not have done that. Moving an injured person can potentially cause even more serious injuries. As tempting as it might be to move them, the injured person should be left alone for medical experts who have the knowledge and equipment to move them properly.

However, since smoke was rising from the car, we were concerned that it could catch fire or burst into flames. I was determined to try to get everybody out of the car and to safety before the ambulances arrived.

The moment I walked upon Dad's car, I sensed a presence of death. It was sickening and eerie—the kind of feeling that makes your hair stand on end. Although I could not see it in the physical realm, I knew that a spirit, perhaps even a death angel, had arrived on the scene. I tried not to believe it, but at the same time I knew what I sensed. Yet in the midst of all this God's comforting presence was there as well.

The young man who hit us was driving a Honda, and it had landed in someone's private driveway. While the car was crushed on all sides and obviously totaled, there seemed to be nothing wrong with him other than a minor leg injury. Since he didn't appear to be badly injured, I thought perhaps he could help us get my family out of the car. He was still sitting behind the wheel when I ran to his car and pleaded, "Could you please help me get my family out of their car?"

Instead of making an attempt to help, he gave me an incredulous look and mumbled, "Hey, man, I can't help you." I kept urging him to please come and help me, but he only sat there and stared at me, as though I was the crazy one for asking.

Though it seemed like an eternity, it was closer to fifteen minutes later when rescue personnel and airlift helicopters began to arrive. They flooded the area with so many lights that the crash scene was lit up like a football field. Using the Jaws of Life, they cut off the top of Dad's car and immediately worked to carefully remove each person and place them on gurneys. Emergency medical technicians performed cardiopulmonary resuscitation on my grandmother Pauline there at the scene.

I'm certain we were a nuisance to the rescue personnel because we kept asking questions and explaining that this was our family from out of town and they didn't know anybody. The gurney that carried Dad was immediately placed in a medical helicopter. I wanted so badly to go alongside him because he was being taken to a hospital in another city that had better emergency facilities, and I could not bear the thought of him being alone there. I felt that I should be with him, but they would not permit me to ride along in the helicopter.

Dad was staring but not focused on anything. He was most likely in shock, definitely in pain, and possibly hemorrhaging internally. I kept encouraging him, "Dad, hang on! You're going to be OK! I'm going to be there. I'll be there with you! Just hang on!"

Matt was also placed on a gurney and airlifted to the children's hospital in a neighboring city. The rest of the family was transported by ambulance to a smaller hospital in our hometown.

Later we learned that Matt had been sitting in the front seat between Mom and Dad. Just before the accident he had tried to coax my mother into persuading us to let him skip school the next day so he could spend time with them.

My mother said to him, "Why don't you lay your head on my lap and we'll talk about it later?" Moments before the crash, he placed his head on her lap. When the vehicle slammed into Dad's car, Matt fell to the floor.

Forty-five minutes earlier we had been eating, laughing, and enjoying one another's company. And now, in a moment's time, our lives were forever changed.

Chapter 3

THE AFTERMATH

B Y THE TIME the rest of us arrived at the emergency room, family members who lived in town had already shown up. I had no clue how they heard about the accident so quickly, since it happened at twelve fifteen on Thursday morning and it was around 1:00 a.m. when we arrived at the emergency room. A dear pastor friend was there as well.

Even though the accident was horrific, I still had confidence that everything was going to be fine. Maybe some would be hospitalized for a while, but surely they all would recover. We waited for word on everyone's conditions, and eventually a doctor came to the emergency room and asked for me.

"Mr. Stone," she said, "I need you to come back here."

Janet and I followed the doctor into a small room, with my pastor and some of my relatives trailing behind us. Still believing that everything was going to be fine, in my most optimistic voice I asked the doctor, "How's my dad?" I just knew she was going to say, "He is in critical condition, but we think he's going to be OK."

Instead she dropped her head and then looked back up at me. "Your dad didn't make it," she said. "He died on the table about an hour ago."

"By himself?" I cried out. "He died by himself?" Then I collapsed.

The doctor then wanted to know, "Who's the little lady in the polka-dot dress?"

I thought aloud, "Who was wearing a polka-dot dress?" Then I remembered, "That's my grandmother."

"She didn't make it either." My grandmother Pauline had been killed on impact when her heart ruptured.

I was not anticipating that news. I screamed. I did not call out to the Lord; I could only scream.

Then the doctor said, "Your son..."

Janet and I both shouted, "No! Not our son! In Jesus's name, no harm will come to our son!"

The doctor delivered the news. "He has severe head injuries and will likely be brain damaged for the rest of his life."

That is when I emotionally fell apart. That news was more than I felt I could bear.

"Your mother is going to be OK," the doctor said, "but she has severe injuries. Your grandfather needed a hundred stitches in his face, but he'll be OK."

Once the doctor had delivered all the news, our pastor friend took me to another room, put his arm around me, and prayed for me and my family. His constant and fervent prayers helped me tremendously that night.

After praying for us, the pastor said that I needed to tell my mother that my dad and her mother had passed away. But I argued, "I can't tell her that. Not now. I can't tell her now."

"You've got to tell her now," he insisted. "The sooner the better."

At that time I didn't understand the importance of telling her right away. But I reluctantly went into my mother's hospital room, where she was lying in severe pain with her face swollen to twice its size and covered with black and blue bruises. With her in that condition, I had to tell my mother that Dad was gone. She asked about her mother. I paused and said, "She didn't make it either, Mom."

My mother's screams could be heard all the way down the hall.

I recalled something Dad said earlier that day, which I did not pay much attention to at the time. He told me, "When we left North Carolina, the closer we came to our destination, the more I had a heavy feeling in my spirit. It almost made me sick to my stomach. I felt like something bad was going to happen. It didn't seem to be coming from me, but from within my spirit."

Dad's heaviness was a spiritual burden—I am certain of it. I will discuss the importance of paying attention to these burdens in a later chapter.

SUSTAINED BY PRAYER

Our son Matt, who was still in a coma, had to be transported to another hospital for a brain scan. We could not bear the thought of losing our son too. It was a blessing beyond words to have the support of so many relatives and church members who gathered at the hospital and prayed for his healing.

Janet felt that she should stay at the hospital with Matt while I returned home to take care of some things. It was emotionally difficult to walk into our home and see my family's luggage, clothes, and personal belongings, knowing that Dad and my grandmother would never return. They had gotten ready for church on Wednesday night, and everything was sitting just as they had left it. Even the atmosphere of our home was filled with the mournful feeling of death.

Our pastor friend drove me home and stayed for two nights so that I would not be there alone. In the corner of our master bedroom was a chair, and the pastor sat in that chair and prayed for us throughout the night.

My cousin Jentezen Franklin called me that first night and said, "Craig, I could sense that the enemy wants to destroy you." Jentezen and other believers prayed for me, and I know it was those prayers and the grace of God that gave me strength to make it through those heart-wrenching times.

The following day the story of the accident appeared in our local newspaper. The headline of the article read, "Highway Patrol Says Driver Crossed Over Center Line." The reporter wrote:

> *The Thursday morning accident which took the lives of two North Carolina residents was apparently caused when one of the vehicles reportedly crossed the center line, according to State Highway Patrol reports.*[1]

The trooper's report indicated that for undetermined reasons the driver lost control of his vehicle and crossed the center line, striking my car and then my dad's.

> *Fred C. Stone, a pastor from Benson, North Carolina, was killed in the accident, as was one other person—Pauline Hunt of Fayetteville, North Carolina, reports said. The Emergency Medical Service transported four others to local hospitals, with one 10-year-old Matthew Stone being flown by the Life Force helicopter to Children's Hospital. The youngster was listed in guarded condition at the facility this morning, according to a hospital spokeswoman.*
>
> *Ninety-year-old Retha Williams of Fayetteville sustained serious injuries in the accident also, reports said. Her condition was upgraded overnight from critical to critical but stable, a hospital spokeswoman said.*
>
> *Two others injured in the accident, Judy Stone and Richard Hunt, both of Fayetteville, were transported to a local hospital with less serious injuries, and were in stable condition on Thursday, according to reports.*[2]

My family had arrived at our home at two o'clock on a Wednesday morning, and within twenty-four hours two of them were gone. Sadly, only a couple of days after arriving in town for what was meant to be a relaxing and enjoyable three-day family gathering, the obituaries of two of my dearest and closest relatives appeared in their local newspapers.

Many of our family members were grief-stricken by my dad's sudden death. It was particularly difficult for his twin brother, Harold. We conducted a joint funeral service for Dad and my grandmother at the C & Adams Street Church of God in Fayetteville the Monday following the accident. The hospital reluctantly released my mother and step-grandfather so they could return to North Carolina to attend the funeral. The funeral director told us that people stood in line for hours to offer condolences to our family. I thought it was important that I stand there and appear strong as I greeted the guests. But inside I felt like I was dying.

After the funeral service I walked away from Dad's gravesite and thought to myself, "Is this all there is? Isn't there more to life besides the grave?"

Once the funerals were over and I returned home, my attention turned to Matt. Janet remained at the hospital with him and even missed the funeral to stay by his side. He was still in a coma and had not been released from intensive care.

Janet was at the hospital almost constantly, but I traveled back and forth. My cousin Ritchie, the brother of Jentezen, came to the hospital and stayed with me all night one night and spent that time praying for me. Again I will say that it was the prayers of God's people and the strength I received from those prayers that carried me through those rough days and weeks.

I had developed another problem, though. I could not drive a car. Somebody had to drive me everywhere I went because I was afraid to get behind the wheel. I could not even sit up in the car without seeing the accident flash before my eyes again. It was like a recording playing over and over in my head. I thought it would never stop. A gentleman in town who owned a funeral home let me borrow a hearse, and my cousins would drive me around as I lay down in the back.

My uncle advised me to see a psychiatrist, telling me, "You can't continue like this. You cannot live in this constant fear." But I never saw a psychiatrist. I simply continued to trust God.

One day I decided to make myself drive, so I got behind the wheel. But fear and apprehension were still constant companions. If I encountered an accident along the highway, I was petrified. As much as I wanted to stop and help the victims, I could not. I'd manage to call 911, but beyond that I froze.

But even in that, I refused to quit driving again. I kept thinking of something I had heard Church of God Bishop Paul Walker say: "I will never be defeated because I will never quit." No matter how difficult or painful the circumstance, I refused to give up. I believed, by the grace of God, that I would get through it. Many times that's all I had to hold on to—the faith that somehow God would bring me through.

I meditated on scriptures such as Philippians 4:13, "I can do all things because of Christ who strengthens me" (MEV), and Psalm 91:1–2, "He who dwells in the shelter of the Most High shall abide under the shadow of the Almighty. I will say of the LORD, 'He is my refuge and my fortress, my God in whom I trust'" (MEV). I would speak those verses out loud, believing that God was with me.

ANOTHER TRAGEDY

Eight weeks after the accident we were confronted with more tragic news. My great-grandmother Retha had been transferred to another hospital where doctors performed surgery. After surgery she seemed to be doing well. Then she contracted a staph infection, which ultimately took her life.

Meanwhile Matt remained in a coma, with doctors offering a bleak prognosis. But friends, family, and people we didn't even know continued to pray. On one particular Friday hundreds of people streamed into the hospital and stood in the hallways to pray for Matt. Surprisingly the hospital personnel did not make them leave or even send them to the chapel.

Then at two in the morning somebody walked into Matt's room and touched him on the head. I like to say that somebody was Jesus. Matt immediately opened his eyes for the first time. He looked at the nurse and said, "I'm hungry."

From that moment on, Matt never looked back. He was healed completely—touched by the power of God. Today he is in perfect health with no physical side effects and no brain damage. He did well in college and is now married and successful. His recovery was indeed a miracle, because the doctors had all but guaranteed he would be brain damaged for life.

We thank God for this healing miracle, and for the many people who stood with us and prayed. We thank Him for moving suddenly and supernaturally to restore Matt, but we learned that God does not heal all wounds in an instant. The wounds of our grief would take much longer to heal. And the ensuing trial only made the healing process that much harder.

Chapter 4

SEEKING JUSTICE

ONCE THINGS SETTLED down after the funerals, and after Matt had returned home and was doing well, we began to reflect on why the accident happened. We lived in a small town with a grapevine that allowed news and gossip to travel faster than e-mail. We kept hearing reports that the twenty-four-year-old driver was intoxicated that night.

We heard that he had been drinking with friends at a bar in a neighboring city the night of the accident, and he had driven nearly all the way home in his father's company car. He was less than a mile from his parents' home when he crossed into the other lane on a curve and hit us.

Someone had picked him up at the accident site and presumably took him home. Nearly two hours after the accident he arrived at the hospital to have the cut on his leg treated. Only then did a highway patrol officer check his blood alcohol level.

Official reports put his blood alcohol level at .09, just under the legal limit, which was then .10 (it is now .08). But both a highway patrol officer and a nurse who was on duty at the hospital that night told us the young man's blood alcohol was actually much higher.

After hearing these stories, our family decided to hire an attorney. We looked for someone in our town, but since the father of the driver was well-known and well-connected, nobody wanted to take the case. So we hired a lawyer from out of state. The local district attorney's office was also involved, and a criminal lawsuit was filed. The goal was to prosecute the driver for assault and vehicular homicide and see him sentenced to jail.

Not long after the accident a retired highway patrol officer I'll call Martin tried to contact me, first by letter then by phone. With all the turmoil at that time, it was awhile before we finally connected. When he finally reached me at our home one day, he said, "I want to talk with you. Can we meet for coffee?" I agreed, and we met at a restaurant downtown.

"I read the tragedy of the Stone family in the newspaper one night," he told me. "Then I threw the paper away. But at three o'clock in the middle of the night something woke me. I got out of bed and went outside to rummage through the garbage can until I found that article."

Martin had already done enough research to be familiar with our whole family, and he was especially concerned about Matthew. After reading the story in the paper, Martin had an incredible desire to help us, and we were happy for all the help we could get.

Right away he began to work diligently, using his connections, resources, and skills to conduct his own investigation. He had plenty of time to work on it, and there is no question he was consumed with this quest. Month after month he documented information according to a timeline, starting with the accident as it occurred at 12:15 a.m. He continued to collect information, even after the trial ended.

Although retired, he had better access to information than did our attorneys. He told *them* what to bring up at trial. Martin was extremely intelligent, precise, detailed, and thorough in his research. He intimidated lawyers, and the attorneys for the defense loathed him.

Throughout the many months that he conducted this investigation, he became a good friend to our family. We all developed a wonderful relationship with him. We were all in agreement that we wanted to see the driver serve time for vehicular homicide.

By the time our fearless and relentless friend had finished collecting investigative material, he had written and organized on paper a stack of information that was perhaps two inches thick. He astonished us with the amount of research he compiled and the data he was able to collect. He caught the smallest details, and day by day he seemed to know exactly what was happening that led up to the trial.

Eventually he sat down with me and said, "Craig, this is so crooked. They are going to get this guy off." I had no way to verify that, but he always seemed to know precisely what he was talking about.

Martin researched and documented every piece of

information. He knew the case had been mishandled. Never should the driver have been permitted to leave the scene of the accident, but I watched as the driver rode away with someone I assumed was his father. I never saw anyone conduct a blood alcohol test at the accident scene. The test was performed at the hospital nearly two hours after the accident.

Someone at the hospital told us that when the driver arrived at the hospital, his blood alcohol level was higher than shown in the report. Because we believed drunk driving—which we felt was the major cause of the accident—would be downplayed at the trial, we asked that individual to testify. But the person refused for fear of losing his job.

As we neared the trial, Martin kept telling us to be forewarned; they were going to get this guy off. He told us that they would not only try to prove that the driver was not intoxicated, but also they would even attempt to raise doubt that he was driving in the wrong lane. We knew that the deck was stacked against us, but we still held hope that the prosecution would present a good case and the jury would be sensible enough to render a just verdict.

OPENING ARGUMENTS

Nearly one year after the accident the case went to trial. The driver had been charged with three counts of criminally negligent homicide and three counts of assault in connection with the accident. The assault charges were related to injuries suffered by Matt, Richard, and my mother. The homicide charges were related to the three deaths.

Six months later the trial began. April 27 was the day of opening arguments, and the trial would last two more days.

During the trial our prosecuting attorneys would attempt to convince jurors that the driver was intoxicated at the time of the fatal accident and prove that his vehicle was in the wrong lane of traffic.

Speaking to the court, the assistant district attorney (ADA) contended that facts substantiated that the driver had taken a test that day and had then met friends at a bar and had three beers. He then drove a friend home from that location before heading back to his parents' home. Around 12:15 a.m. he was involved in the accident.[1]

The ADA said the driver registered a .09 on blood alcohol content. Legally drunk in the state was .10 (today it is .08), and the prosecuting attorney said his blood alcohol level was likely much higher at the time of the accident because he wasn't tested until two hours after the collision. "It is not the case of whether [he] meant to kill them," the prosecutor argued, "but was his conduct reckless?"[2]

The defense attorney disagreed that the driver was negligently reckless, arguing instead that he had not slept much the previous few nights because he was studying for final exams. The driver's attorney agreed that his client did, in fact, meet with friends at a bar near the university, and he did drink three beers.

The attorney said that his client realized he was tired and did not need to stay and drink any more. He claimed that the driver attempted to keep himself awake as much as possible by rolling down the window and turning up the radio.

Just as our friend Martin had warned, along with intoxication, the actual point of impact would be at issue in the trial. The ADA told the court that the driver was in the opposite lane, headed toward oncoming traffic. His vehicle struck our vehicle and then continued into the pathway of Dad's vehicle. Indeed, this is exactly how the accident happened.

But the driver's attorney told the jury that he would raise reasonable doubts about which lane of traffic his client's car was in when the accident occurred.

The state trooper who arrived at the scene of the accident had called for assistance from another trooper who went to the hospital to get a blood alcohol sample. This sample was not taken until two hours after the accident and about three hours after the driver left the bar.[3]

Another trooper took the stand and admitted that he could smell alcohol on the driver's breath. But he testified that during his interview with the driver at 4:00 a.m., "If I had not heard him say he had had three beers, I saw no indicators of intoxication."[4]

Yet another state trooper, who was the traffic reconstructionist, gave the most damaging testimony. He said he analyzed the scene the morning following the accident and concluded that the first impact occurred in the northbound lane of traffic. He based that conclusion on evidence such as debris on the roadway and marks left on the road, including one that he contended was made by the left front wheel of our vehicle going flat upon collision with the driver's vehicle.[5]

He corroborated what we all knew—that the driver was in our lane of traffic when he hit both my car and Dad's.

The driver's attorney attempted to get the traffic reconstructionist to raise doubt in the minds of jurors by claiming there was a possibility that one or both cars were lifted upon impact, which would have caused a mark later in the collision instead of where the first impact occurred. But the trooper stayed with his conclusion and said that he found no evidence of either vehicle being raised by the impact.[6]

The prosecution presented their witness, the state's chief medical examiner, who discussed how alcohol affects individuals. For a person of the driver's weight, if that person's blood alcohol content registered .09 at 2:00 a.m., then at 1:00 a.m. the reading would have been around .105. And it would have been .12 at midnight, when the accident occurred.[7]

In 1993 a reading of .10 constituted legal intoxication, and a person would be deemed unable to drive in our state. The medical examiner said some people can exhibit a normal appearance at the .10 limit and over, though in his opinion, everyone who registers over .08 has had their reason, time, and judgment affected.[8]

When it was my turn to testify, the driver's attorney accused me of lying when I said that the oncoming car was in my lane.

I replied, "Sir, I'm not lying to you. I'm telling you the truth."

He even accused me of talking to several witnesses and telling them what to say, which was complete nonsense.

Defense testimony included the driver's dad, who had arrived to take him from the scene of the accident, as well as the friends who were with him that night at the bar. His friends swore under oath that the driver had consumed only one beer. When our attorney asked them how many drinks they had consumed, none of them could say. Yet they all claimed to know how much the defendant had consumed.

The majority of the defense's testimony was from a former professor of engineering at a local university that was, coincidentally, the driver's undergraduate alma mater. He discussed the accident scene and said that he felt the front edge of our vehicle was "slightly across the center line," while adding that from his analysis, the driver's vehicle was "close to the center line, but not across it." This man tried to convince the jury that, if the accident occurred in the northbound lane as both the state trooper who first arrived on the scene and I contended, the collision would have caused the driver's car to miss my dad's car completely.[9]

In cross examination the ADA did get this former professor to admit that he was not on the scene the morning of the April accident, as the trooper had been, and that the professor actually performed his analysis two months later in mid-July when there were no more marks or debris on the road. But this man would not change his opinion. He said, "I think that the second impact would also not have happened if the two tires [on our vehicle and on the driver's] had not ruptured." He went on to say that the side-swiping collision continued, and then both vehicles began rotating, ours clockwise and the driver's counterclockwise into Dad's car.[10]

That man's testimony was absurd. Not only did he look at the accident scene two and a half months later, when there was nothing to look at, but he also stated that our car rotated clockwise. We know that our car did not rotate. We were 100 percent awake and aware that we were in the ditch, headed toward a front-end collision with a utility pole.

VERDICT RENDERED

The next day the driver took the stand in his own defense and stated that he did not remember what occurred during the accident. When asked if he perceived himself to be a danger in drinking and driving, he said, "Absolutely not. If I had, I would have stayed at [a friend's house] or called my parents."[11]

The prosecution told the jury that they would have to resolve the issue of whether or not the driver's conduct led to the accident. Did he understand the risk? Did his actions indicate that he knew the dangers of driving drunk and sleepy?

In reference to the location of the crash the prosecution told the jury that evidence pointed to the driver being in the opposite lane of traffic. He stressed that the only eyewitnesses to the accident (besides the driver, who could not remember the accident) said I exclaimed prior to the accident, "That car is in our lane!" Every witness who had been in our vehicle affirmed that statement.

In his closing statements the defense attorney said the testimony in the trial should lead the jury to doubt the driver's guilt. He said his client was not impaired, pointing out that he drove from the bar and was almost home before having a wreck. Regarding his blood alcohol level, the driver's attorney reminded the jury that witnesses testified that, except for the smell of alcohol as they neared the driver, he was cooperative and alert when they spoke with him two to four hours after the accident.

The arguments ended, and the jury was sent to consider the testimony. They deliberated for three hours and twenty minutes before returning with a verdict of not guilty on all counts of both assault and criminally negligent homicide. When the acquittal was rendered, emotions ran high in both families, from the relief of the driver's family to the astonishment and pain of ours.

After the trial ended, the defense attorney was quoted by reporters as saying, "This is a verdict which I wish had never had to be rendered.... This was a tragic accident. It is an accident which has resulted in great pain for everybody involved."[12]

Awhile after the trial ended, this same defense attorney came to me outside the courtroom and put his hands on my shoulders. Using foul language that I won't repeat, he seemed to suggest that he was just doing what he had to do in the courtroom.

Even before the trial ended, we knew that Martin had been correct in his assessment; the defense had attacked the evidence and undermined the obvious fact that the driver was traveling in the wrong lane.

The jury was comprised of quite a few young people, which probably worked in the driver's favor. I imagine they would be sympathetic to someone their own age. But the biggest boon for the driver was that his attorney was able to successfully plant doubt in the minds of the jurors. Attorneys know that questioning important details is the best way to plant reasonable doubt in the minds of jurors. And the jury is given instructions that, if you have reasonable doubt, you should not vote to convict.

Many of my aunts and uncles were present during the trial. One aunt in particular is someone to whom I pay attention when she speaks because she is a very wise woman. During the trial process she affirmed what I already knew. "Craig, this is stacked," she said. "I can feel it in this courtroom." Everybody sensed that something was not right, but she had a more keen awareness than any of the rest.

From the time of the accident until after the trial—and even up to this day—we have seen no remorse from the driver. During the trial my brother and I were in the restroom when the driver walked in. I was thinking to myself, "My brother and I could mess you up right now." We were in an ideal position to beat him to a pulp, which is exactly what I wanted to do. But had we done that, we would have caused a mistrial, and we would have been the ones going to jail. The Lord helped me control my emotions and be smart enough to restrain myself from pulverizing the guy.

For years it bothered me that the driver showed no

remorse for his actions. I did talk to his father, who at least showed concern for what his son had done. I believe this tragedy would have been easier for the family to deal with in the long run had the driver expressed some sorrow for the events that killed three people and seriously injured three others.

But I learned after being tortured by grief and unforgiveness for years that my healing couldn't depend on what the driver did or didn't do. I would have to make a choice to forgive. But in those initial years after the trial, *forgive* wasn't a word I was ready to hear.

Chapter 5

LIFE GOES ON?

THE TRIAL WAS over, and so was a great part of my life. Or so it seemed. In our large and close-knit family many were affected by these three deaths, and regretfully a few are yet to recover.

My mother had lost her husband and her mother on the same day, and then her grandmother several weeks later. She experienced the loss of no longer being the pastor's wife, since now that Dad was gone, the church needed a new pastor. The North Carolina state bishop for the denomination showed great kindness and compassion to her through this transition. Then she was faced with the emptiness of living alone at their home in Fayetteville and grieving the loss of three of her dearest and closest family members.

After the accident our children did not want to let Janet and me out of their sight. They clung to us as never before. It was difficult for the two of us to comprehend the circumstances, so there was no possible way we could explain it to them. One day their granddad was visiting their home and playing with them, and before the night was over, he was gone. No doubt they also feared losing us as they had lost him.

About five years after the accident I once again was preaching at the same church where I preached when the accident occurred. After the service we had dinner at the same Shoney's restaurant we had visited on that fateful night. Jonathan sat down with us but later left the table. We noticed that he had been gone awhile and still had not returned, so we thought we should look for him. I found him in the restroom, sitting in the corner crying. He had been six years old when he last saw his granddad alive at this restaurant. Five years later he found himself dealing with the memory.

Then, my precious wife, Janet, had the challenge of living with me. The sudden and tragic death of loved ones did not become easier to deal with just because my family was long buried, the trial was over, and others seemed to have moved on with life. Those who suffer through such loss will find themselves experiencing painful grief.

In the midst of all this grief it is impossible to crawl into a hole and disappear. Most people have only one choice, and that is to keep working and putting forth the effort and appearance of a normal life. For me, a normal life meant preaching the message of the gospel of Jesus Christ. It was not easy to stand behind a pulpit and preach while dealing with an overpowering sense of grief and anger. Not only was I mourning the loss of my family, but I was also angry over the outcome of the trial. Live with anger long enough, and it can turn into an all-consuming rage.

I continued to preach because this was my occupation and I had to support my family. But I went through the motions of preaching. I stood in someone else's church by invitation as an evangelist, but I felt empty. Everything seemed mechanical.

Even as I tried to engage in ministry, I was still fiercely angry at the young man driving the car that night. I was angry because he never once said, "I'm sorry," and never once expressed an ounce of remorse. Could the guy not even manage a simple heartfelt apology?

I was angry that this young man was able to walk from the courtroom a free man instead of serving time in jail where I felt he belonged. He was free to carry on his life as though nothing happened while the rest of us were left to pick up and put back together the broken pieces.

Dad's death was especially difficult for my brother and me. He was gone—his own life snuffed out too soon. It was difficult to witness the manner in which his death was minimized by people in that courtroom. Who was my dad to these people? Dad was an incredible man who left an amazing legacy, but to those people he was nobody.

Justice was not served, so I was angry. It was shocking to watch the judicial system in action. The facts were twisted to create doubt, and I believe some witnesses lied outright. For many involved, this seemed to be just another case to win, whatever the cost. The end justifies the means.

WHY, GOD?

Such were the thoughts racing through my mind after the trial. And I confess that I also was angry at God. Over and over I asked, "Why, God? Why did You allow this to happen? Why?" I was thirty-two years old at the time and would never again talk with or spend time with my dad. He would never again play with his grandchildren whom he loved dearly. He would never know his great-grandchildren.

I knew the Lord could have stopped that accident. He could have protected my family. Or He could have healed every one of them. Instead, God let my family die while the other driver walked away with a cut on his leg.

I knew it was wrong to be angry at God. But I was angry at God.

Guilt was ever present because I thought that I was partly to blame for the accident. Had I succeeded in convincing my family to stay home from church that night, they would not have died. Had I not been in a hurry to get home that night, I might not have taken the shortcut. Had we left Shoney's ten minutes later, the guy would have already made the turn to go home by the time we reached the curve. Had we not visited Shoney's at all, we would have been home before he even left the bar. These thoughts were constant companions that battered my mind.

Even as I kept preaching, I continued to question God, my faith, and everything I stood for. I asked myself, "Do I believe all of this because it's what I have been taught? Or is it truly real?"

Given time, unresolved anger will turn to bitterness. It seemed that I could do nothing to deal with losing Dad and seeing the driver go free. Thoughts raced over and over in my head. And the more I entertained those thoughts, the more I allowed rage and bitterness to take root and grow. My life became consumed with hatred for the man I considered responsible for the deaths of my family members and for the people involved in helping him to walk free.

Finally I concluded there was only one way to fix this. I would get revenge. I would deal with this guy once and for all. I didn't believe he deserved to walk free. So I made plans to avenge their deaths.

I had been preaching a revival and was driving back home along the interstate. I had a gun in my car. And I kept thinking about shooting the guy. How spiritual is that? I had just preached a revival, and now I was thinking about shooting someone.

These thoughts controlled my mind as I left the revival and drove toward home. Nobody else knew what I was thinking, but God did. And in the car that day He arrested me, stopping me in my tracks. He clearly spoke to me and said, "How can you preach and tell others about forgiveness if you will not forgive? I cannot take you any further in ministry until you get past this."

I pulled my car to the side of the road and stopped. I threw my hands in the air and confessed to Him, "Lord, I cannot do this on my own. You know that I hate this guy and I want to hurt him. You know I cannot forgive him. But I give it to You because only You can get me through this. You have to help me."

Only when I committed to putting it all in God's hands and letting Him do His work in me did the healing process begin. I started to work through this bitterness and reconstruct my life.

Throughout this time Janet was a tremendous help and support. Circumstances like this can break a marriage apart, but I am thankful that this made us stronger. Even though today she says it was hard to deal with, she encouraged me, prayed for me, and prayed with me. She traveled with me to revivals as much as possible, especially in the summer months when the children were out of school. We were committed to our marriage and to each other.

Janet admits that it's hard to know what to say to someone who is hurting because you don't know how the person is going to receive it. An innocent comment can cause unintended hurt. People blame each other. She now tells people that the best thing to do is keep quiet when you want to say something you think could hurt the person or be taken the wrong way. Say only things that are uplifting and encouraging. And pray. Those were tough days for Janet and me, but we were committed to dealing with the tough times. And we came through it one day at a time.

One thing that helped was exercise; we started playing tennis together. The whole family went to the tennis court, and that was therapy for me. It gave me something else to focus on, and I enjoyed going to this particular park each week with my family. There is also a physiological reason exercise of this sort is therapy. Exercise helps the blood flow to the brain, which in turn helps the limbic system.[1]

From personal experience I can say that exercise not only occupies the mind, but it also helps correct chemical disruptions in the brain. Research shows that, chemically, the brain problem becomes worse when you do as I did and blame yourself, or focus on negativity, the person who committed the wrong, and the years you will not have with the person you lost.[2]

You cannot spend time dwelling on the problem and allowing it to occupy space in your head. When you do, it will make you feel like you are going crazy. Many times my cousin Jentezen said to me, "You almost lost your mind."

I replied, "Yes, I did. And I got it renewed."

I started speaking the words I'd heard from Paul Walker every day: "I will never be defeated because I will never quit." And I began to meditate on scriptures that addressed what I was going through, not only Psalm 91:1–2 and Philippians 4:13, but also John 8:36, "If the Son sets you free, you shall be free indeed" (MEV), and 2 Corinthians 1:3, which says the Lord is the God of all comfort.

Change happened slowly, day by day, as though God was peeling away one layer at a time. I was not an overnight success. My life was still a roller coaster, and I dealt with depression. I had always been a positive person, but this destroyed my positive outlook for a long time.

But I thought of what Jentezen told me: "Craig, I could sense that the enemy wants to destroy you." I knew this meant that the enemy was hoping to destroy my emotions, my spiritual life, and my ministry.

Would I let this happen? I had to make a choice. I

could get this out of my spirit and not allow the enemy to defeat and destroy me, or I could let the enemy win and my life would be over. I would forever be remembered as the evangelist who got wiped out after his family was killed in a car accident.

Before the accident happened, it seemed that we had reached a high point in ministry. We were ready to go worldwide. But this knocked me off my feet. There were years on the dark side of the desert where I felt like everything was over. Because I was hurting and depressed, I felt like I was being a hypocrite. I was on the path of giving up, but quitting is not something God wants us to do. He is not against us. God will never be against us. Did this accident have to happen? I cannot answer that. But it did, and nothing can ever be done to reverse it. I had to move forward.

LEARNING TO FORGIVE

With the Lord's help I was able to forgive the driver, and throughout this book I will show you how that happened. But for now I will say that forgiveness is not about forgetting, because you will never completely forget. You can, however, stop rehearsing it over and over in your mind. One of the most difficult issues for me after the accident and for the next two years was the fact that the driver did not spend one night in jail. It was difficult knowing that three wonderful people were gone and he did not have to pay for anything he did. I carried that anger, hurt, and unforgiveness toward him for years, and I did not have one moment of peace that entire time.

When I gave all of that anger, hurt, and unforgiveness

over to the Lord that day in the car, I got freedom. I was no longer defining my life by the hurt I experienced, and instead of seeking vengeance myself, I put that in God's hands. Romans 12:19 tells us that vengeance belongs to the Lord; He will repay. I chose to take Him at His Word, and when I did, a weight seemed to fall off.

If you want peace in your life, you absolutely cannot hate the person who harmed you, nor can you continue to justify your wrong attitude by playing the blame game. You cannot desire to harm the person and seek revenge. I had that desire at one time, but I do not anymore. Yes, I believe the driver was irresponsible when he decided to drive home after drinking that night, even if a jury didn't consider him legally intoxicated at the time of the accident. I still have no tolerance for those who drink and drive. Anybody who gets behind the wheel of a car and drives while intoxicated is endangering every person he encounters on the highway. If he causes an accident and kills someone, he has committed homicide with a car.

I will discuss forgiveness throughout this book, but for now let me say that the primary reason to forgive is because God tells us to forgive. Men with clenched fists cannot shake hands, and it is essential that we learn to express true forgiveness with open hands and open hearts. You are never more like Jesus Christ than when you say to someone who has wronged, harmed, or crushed you, "I forgive you." Those are three of the most powerful words you will ever speak.

To forgive is to show true Christlikeness, while harboring hatred, malice, bitterness, and unforgiveness toward someone causes you to become more like the adversary. To be more like Christ or more like the enemy is your choice. But I pray you will choose to release forgiveness and refuse to be bound in chains the enemy wants to wrap around us.

It is not possible to pray as you should when you live with unforgiveness because it blocks the channel between you and God. Forgive, keep the Lord first, and stay in right relationship with Him. I have been in the place where I neglected all three, and I almost let the enemy succeed in his efforts to wipe me out.

It is easy to become angry and bitter, and then spend the rest of your life blaming the perpetrator for making you angry and bitter. But consider the biblical story of Job. He lost everything except his wife and his life, and still he said, "Though He slay me, yet will I trust in Him" (Job 13:15, MEV).

Whatever God wants me to do in the second half of my life, I want to do it. And since I wanted to obey God, I had to deal with the anger, forgive, and move on. There was unforgiveness among other family members as well, but I could not control them. I could only work on myself. I couldn't preach to them about unforgiveness when I was not being a good example myself.

Even when I was living with so much anger and preaching those empty sermons, as a minister I knew in my heart that I could not keep going through the motions. So I told the Lord, "If You will give me back the anointing, I will never preach without it again. I've preached with it and I've preached without it. And I don't want to preach without it anymore."

The anointing of the Holy Spirit returned and the channel opened again. I have been on the other side, and I will not go back. One minister said to me, "You mean after all that, you're still serving God? It's a wonder you didn't go the other way."

I replied, "You'd better believe I'm still serving God. I'm sure the enemy wanted me to go the other way. But by the grace of God, the people who love me, and the power of prayer, I'm still serving God. To Him I give the glory."

The Lord will use your circumstances to help others if you will overcome and obey. Jentezen and I filmed several programs together on drunk driving, and the response was incredible. Today, if somebody in our church goes through a similar tragedy, I am able to help that person through it. I go to court with him or her if necessary. It is good to know that the Lord is using my own painful experiences to help other people make progress.

We all will experience adversity because it is part of life on this earth. Will we choose to allow grief and negative, harmful emotions to consume us? Will we choose to live and die with unforgiveness? Or will we ask the Lord to change our hearts and allow the process to teach us important, life-changing messages?

One of the lessons we learn is to consider how we might have handled things differently, both as a benefit to ourselves in the future and as wisdom to impart to others. We learn about forgiving ourselves as well as the person we held captive in our mind. And always we hope to look past the wrong and see the humanity of the person who harmed us. That always leads us down the path of asking our heavenly Father to help us extend forgiveness to that person. By the end of the process we more fully understand tragedy, ourselves, God, and eternity.

Through the rest of this book I will address the lessons I have learned as I dealt with grief, depression, anger, and unforgiveness. Know that only by making the right choices throughout this process can we ensure the enemy's defeat and our ultimate victory.

Chapter 6

OVERCOMING GRIEF

I N 1956 C. S. Lewis married an American poet. After four happy years of marriage his wife died of cancer, and Lewis wrote about his grief. He observed several things. He wrote that the absence of the person who has died is like the sky spread over everything. Grief feels like fear—with the same stomach flutters and restlessness. Lewis wanted others around him, but he wished they wouldn't talk to him. Grief brings laziness—a loathing of even the slightest effort. An unhappy man wants distractions like the sleepy man who wants an extra blanket at night but would rather lie shivering than get up and find one. This is why the lonely become untidy and even dirty and disgusting.

Lewis wrote that part of misery is the misery's shadow or reflection: the fact that you don't merely suffer but have to keep on thinking about the fact that you suffer. "I not only live each endless day in grief, but live each day thinking about living each day in grief,"[1] he wrote. Lewis also said that you will ask yourself: Where is God, and why has He forsaken me?

Every person who lives long enough and loves people will inevitably, at some desperate point in life, experience grief. When tragedy strikes, grief hammers us like a battering ram. God created us to experience a range and depth of feelings, so any personal loss or the death of one we love is guaranteed to affect our emotions.

Unexpected losses are often the worst, because there is no time to prepare for the shock of losing a loved one. But expected or unexpected, we still miss the person, and we will experience times of longing to see our loved one again, to be in his presence, or to simply hear her voice or laughter.

In these difficult times the overwhelming power of grief can seem to consume us. I have heard stories of people who lost their children to tragic events, and I cannot imagine what those parents must go through. But at the same time I have heard them speak of how this was an opportunity for them to experience God's grace. No matter what we go through, God is still in complete control, and He still has us in the palm of His hand. Psalm 30:5 tells us that weeping may endure for a night, but joy comes in the morning.

Grief is a normal reaction to loss. People *expect* us to weep over the person's death and miss him when he's gone. Grief is not an emotional or mental disorder that should be treated with prescription drugs. Rather than being concerned about the person who grieves, we should be concerned about the person who does not.

Grief isn't something we will overcome in a day; I held on to my grief for a long time—five or six years—and I wasn't better for it. I was tormented by guilt and anger. I now realize that it is possible to grieve yet experience the peace and comfort of God promised in His Word.

STAGES OF GRIEF

Some psychologists define the stages of grief as denial, anger, bargaining, depression, and acceptance. Other psychologists add the stages of pain or guilt, and working through the problem, which leads to acceptance and hope.

Most people will pass through one or more stages of grief before reaching emotional healing. The key is to pass through. If we remain stuck at one stage, it becomes difficult to move past our grief. If we never move past the stage that is holding us bound, grief will consume us. Yes, there is a time to mourn, but there is also a time to recover our joy. Ecclesiastes 3:4 tells us that there is a time to weep and a time to laugh, a time to mourn and a time to dance.

When we experience an unexpected loss, our first emotions are shock, numbness, and disbelief. When I was confronted with the news of the death of my dad and grandmother, the first thought that crossed my mind was, "This cannot be happening." My mind was in denial.

Grief causes us to feel sadness and emptiness, and it could even bring with it excruciating physical pain. All of these feelings are difficult but normal. Denying them, ignoring them, or drowning them in alcohol, drugs, or anything else that temporarily numbs the pain will only make life worse in the long run. Trying to maintain a brave front for the benefit of family and friends, as I did at the funeral, is unwise and pointless. It is OK if we cry and tell people how we feel. If we never acknowledge the pain, it might never go away.

Perhaps you will do as I did and place guilt upon yourself, thinking that had you done something differently, you could have prevented the loss. If I had not accepted the revival invitation, if I had closed the revival a day earlier, if I had chosen a different route home—if, if, if— then maybe my family would still be alive.

We might be plagued by words that play over and over in our heads—words we wish we had said while we still had the chance. We might face guilt because we failed to deal with unresolved problems in the relationship. The worst guilt for a believer is in knowing that we could have shared the gospel and perhaps led that person to Christ before he died, but we never made the effort. Now we must live with the knowledge that the person might have died lost.

Another emotion we could experience is anger. There is righteous anger, and then there is unrighteous anger. Righteous anger helps us see injustice and take action to make wrong things right. Unrighteous anger is harmful; it makes us want to get even and hurt somebody so the person will pay for the wrong he or she committed.

When my family learned that the driver had been drinking the night of the accident, we fought for justice. We were even angrier when he walked away unpunished. Anger in itself is not a sin; it is our reaction to the anger that can cause us to sin. My own reaction, which led to thoughts of shooting the guy, was an example of sinning in anger.

In the anger stage we ask ourselves questions such as: Why did this happen? Who is to blame? A drunk driver? The medical community? Another family member? At this stage we look for someone to blame and wonder how we can make that person pay.

Sometimes we are angry at God. Why did He let this happen? He could have stopped it; why didn't He?

Some even blame the person who died. Did the person die of a condition that could have been diagnosed and treated early enough to extend or save his life? Did the person commit suicide? Was the death caused by the person's own careless actions?

Survivors feel betrayed. They question why this individual would engage in an action that resulted in his death. Feeling abandoned because of the deceased person's selfishness, the survivors want to know how that loved one could just leave them like that.

Even if nobody was to blame, those who feel the pain of grief believe they must blame *somebody*. Psychologists say that anger is a defensive mechanism that helps us deflect our pain.[2] Placing blame is one way the mind deals with such overpowering emotions. Families have been torn apart and couples have divorced over this kind of pointless blame game.

If there is any possible way to reverse the loss— such as in the case of a divorce or failed relationship— the grief-stricken person might use bargaining tactics to bring the person back. Bargaining says that if you will come back, I will never again do whatever caused you to leave.

At the bargaining stage people sometimes return to the relationship, only to be hurt and rejected each time they return, thereby starting the grief process all over again. Unless God changes someone from the inside, it is likely that those promises made in the bargaining process will be temporary.

One potentially serious side effect of grief is depression, which we will discuss at length in the next chapter. We can easily be overcome with depression when we focus on our loss and everything we are missing. Choosing isolation is one way people deal with emptiness, despair, and depression. Friends and family will try to speak words of encouragement over us at this stage, but their efforts seldom help.

After my dad and grandmothers died, I often wanted to be by myself, because people distracted me from thinking about the things that had caused me so much hurt and were making me so angry. Being alone isn't a bad idea in and of itself, but if we're not careful, grief can become a spirit that attacks us. We can begin to wallow in our grief and end up in despair, thinking there is no hope for the future. Overcoming grief is something we do day by day as we choose to face our pain and move *through* it instead of allowing ourselves to wallow in it.

If we allow ourselves to get stuck in grief, physical problems can manifest in our bodies—nausea, weight loss or weight gain, insomnia, various aches and pains, and even serious or deadly illnesses. Science and medicine have proven that the mind has a profound effect on the body. Chronic stress, anger, depression, or even repression of your feelings can cause the heart to race, the digestive system to slow, the blood pressure and cholesterol to rise, harmful hormones to be released into the bloodstream, and the immune system to become suppressed. Major organ systems can deteriorate prematurely.[3] For our own well-being, we cannot allow symptoms of grief to continue indefinitely.

In the midst of our grief we might desire to crawl into a hole and disappear, but that is nearly impossible. Most of us have only one choice, which is to keep going about the routines of life.

I had to keep preaching the gospel whether I felt like it or not. It was not easy to stand behind a pulpit and speak while dealing with such overpowering emotions that seemed to drain the very life from me. Every action seemed mechanical; every sermon seemed contrived.

Given enough time, grief and depression will lift if you do not allow yourself to wallow in grief forever. One day you will realize that the grief is fading. You will pick up the broken pieces of your life and start mending them. You will accept that what's done is done, and there is nothing you can do to reverse it. You will move forward. The sun peeks through the clouds and you realize that life can be good again despite your loss. Some psychologists consider this a working-through and reconstruction process.

Prayer—along with a support system of family, friends, and other believers—will give you the strength you need to overcome your grief and find hope again. And we cannot neglect the importance of giving our problems to God. After all, He is the healer—not just of our physical bodies, but of our entire being, including our emotions.

STRATEGIES FOR OVERCOMING GRIEF

Through the rest of this chapter I will address some of the ways psychologists suggest we overcome grief without resorting to emotion-numbing medications.

Don't bury the pain

We cannot simply push pain out of our mind and expect to move on with life. This does not make the problem go away, because the pain is still hidden in the back of our minds.

Repression, or trying not to think about it, does not help and can cause severe damage to the physical body. Repression of anger is particularly damaging. Medical doctors say that angry people—including those who repress anger—are the most stressed out, and they suffer from a greater number of physical ailments. Lab specialists can read the chemical composition of your blood and tell if you are angry because of the cortisol levels in your blood. Excessive cortisol damages many of the major organs in your body.[4]

Anger, even when repressed, also harms you emotionally and spiritually. Experts in the field of psychology say that it is not reality, but your perception of reality, that affects your body and emotions. We are able to change our perception by looking at the situation through a different set of lenses. In other words, we cannot change reality, but we can change the way we perceive our circumstances.

Reading the Bible and meditating on what it says will help us to see the situation differently because this renews the mind. Also, praying and asking the Lord to guide us through the trouble is vital when dealing with problems. This was vital in keeping me strong, both spiritually and emotionally. I meditated daily on God's Word, reminding myself that He would see me through. And in those times when the grief was so intense I didn't think I would make it, I would pray. Sometimes I was unable to utter much more than, "Help, Lord!" On a few occasions the grief was so intense I called trusted friends and asked them to pray with me, and because of those prayers the oppression would lift. Don't underestimate the power of prayer and meditating on God's Word.

Express your grief

Discover your own meaningful ways to deal with your emotions and pain. Some people keep a journal. Others talk to a trusted friend, pastor, or counselor. Some even write a letter that expresses the things they didn't have a chance to say.

Consider getting involved in an organization related to the cause of death. It can be comforting to find others who have dealt with similar circumstances and hear them share how they coped with their own tragedy. For example, I joined MADD—Mothers Against Drunk Driving. There I learned that every fifty minutes someone dies in a drunk-driving accident. The average drunk driver has driven while intoxicated eighty times before his first arrest.[5]

Tragedy can even lead to career or legislative changes. In 1981 six-year-old Adam Walsh was abducted from a Florida mall and later asphyxiated and decapitated. As a result, his father became a victim's rights advocate and host of a television program called *America's Most Wanted*. John Walsh not only helped bring notorious criminals to justice, but he also changed the way authorities search for missing children. John's efforts led to the 2006 signing of the Adam Walsh Child Protection Act.[6]

As horrible as the circumstances might be, ask the Lord to help you find a way to bring something good out of the tragedy. Many organizations were founded and legislation passed because someone was motivated enough to help others deal with similar problems.

Be aware of trigger events

Make plans for dealing with situations that might trigger painful emotions. Holidays, birthdays, anniversaries, and vacations can be trigger events. A trigger event also might be an upcoming wedding ceremony, knowing that you will not have your mother or father present.

One of the best things you can do is talk about the upcoming event and decide in advance how you will handle it. During these times try not to be alone, as this can cause you to become depressed if you allow yourself to dwell on your thoughts.

Keep the memory of the person alive

Often family and friends try to avoid talking about the person, believing that reliving memories will be too painful. In retrospect, people often realize that talking about their loved one, recalling memories, laughing about humorous events, reminiscing over family photos, or showing old family videos helps the grief-stricken person tremendously. They realize that, although the person is out of sight, he or she is not forgotten.

Don't think you should "just get over it"

Medical research shows that the deep limbic system of the brain promotes bonding, controls emotions, and stores highly charged emotional memories. When you are strongly bonded to someone and that person dies, the neurochemical bond is broken and the deep limbic system of the brain is disrupted. Grief feels physical because grief activates the pain centers of the brain, which are located near the limbic system.[7] Pain caused by grief is not imaginary; it is very real. So don't think you should just get over it—and don't allow anyone to make you think you should do so.

If you know someone who is experiencing grief, I urge you not to tell them, "Just get over it." First, they will resent your lack of empathy. Second, by telling them to get over it, you are telling them to do something nearly impossible, which is to take control of neurochemicals in their brain. Help them by listening and letting them talk, or by offering to become involved in some activity. Pray for them. But do not try to force them to "get over" their grief. They will cope with the loss in their own way and in their own time. If the mourning continues for months or even years, and the individual is becoming depressed and unable to function, encourage that person to seek professional help. This brings me to my next point.

Know when to seek help

If you find that grief is consuming your life and leading to stress, family problems, persistent depression, or suicidal thoughts, it is time to talk to a counselor, a pastor, or some other compassionate person who can help. Pay attention to family and friends who notice that grief is overtaking you. When I was grieving, it never occurred to me to visit a counselor; I thought God could take care of everything—and He can. The best counselor is our heavenly Father. In the words of the old hymn, we can take our troubles to the Lord and leave them there. But I believe God can use Christian counselors to help us through our grieving process. So if you are struggling to cope with grief, don't think you have to go it alone. Seek help from a reputable, Spirit-filled counselor.

Beware of destructive behaviors

Do not resort to illegal drug use, alcohol abuse, promiscuity, or anything else that is sinful, destructive, or addictive. This will only compound your problem, as these things mask emotions—and they do so only temporarily. When the high wears off, the grief, anger, and depression will return along with the added troubles brought by destructive behaviors. Avoid compounding the pain. Talk with someone who can help you, and let the Lord be your healer.

Take care of yourself

Make sure you get enough sleep, exercise, and proper nutrition. Your immune system will already be compromised by the emotional toll you are under, and taking care of your body will help prevent or reduce illnesses and immune system disorders.

When you are not sleeping well, you lose focus and motivation. Lack of sleep makes you more irritable and depressed and causes you to have less energy.[8] Sleep deprivation also causes decreased activity in some parts of the brain.[9]

Exercise helps get your mind off your problems, which I learned when my family and I began to play tennis together. Exercise calms worry and anxiety, helps you sleep better, enhances your mood, and gives you a general feeling of well-being. When your heart pumps because you are engaged in some form of exercise, your brain releases chemicals that make you feel better. In some cases moderate exercise, particularly cardiovascular activity, has proved as effective as prescription medication in treating depression. And it has no harmful side effects.[10]

Proper nutrition is always important but even more so when you are under stress. Our bodies and brains continually renew cells, and food fuels cell growth and regeneration. The foods we eat affect our health and cognitive abilities. Eat healthy foods. Drink plenty of water to hydrate your body and brain, because dehydration can cause the release of stress hormones. It is important to take care of yourself.[11]

Laugh

Even if you have to force yourself to laugh, do it anyway. Read funny comics or watch comedies. Researchers say that laughter counteracts stress and is good for your immune system. It is physically impossible to be stressed when you are laughing.[12]

Be thankful

Practice gratitude every day. This is not easy when we are dealing with grief. It takes discipline and obedience to God's Word to be thankful in times of trouble. Expressing thankfulness improves our outlook and, according to brain scans, improves the condition of the brain.[13]

It is even possible to be thankful for the person you lost. In the movie *Courageous* one of the characters asked a powerful question: Are we going to be angry for the time we didn't have, or grateful for the time we did have?[14]

Do not languish in grief

If we do not overcome our grief—and especially our anger—we might find ourselves living with bitterness and unforgiveness—and they make terrible roommates. I have seen this in my own life as well as in the lives of family members. Do not allow grief, anger, bitterness, and unforgiveness to wreck your health and relationships.

Forgive

If you are grieving over circumstances caused by someone else's behavior, have you forgiven that person? Is there someone you refuse to forgive? Is there someone you are convinced you cannot forgive? Must you forgive them?

Forgiveness is an often misunderstood yet vitally important action. What does it mean to forgive? Forgiveness is easy to talk about, but as C. S. Lewis said in *Mere Christianity*, "Everyone says forgiveness is a lovely idea until they have something to forgive."[15]

Forgiveness is so vital that much of this book is devoted to this topic. We will examine forgiveness biblically, relationally, emotionally, and physically. If you or people you know are holding grudges and harboring unforgiveness, I urge you to learn from those chapters and allow the Lord to transform your life.

Hand your grief to the Lord

Isaiah 53:4–5 tells us, "Surely He has borne our griefs and carried our sorrows; yet we esteemed Him stricken, smitten by God, and afflicted. But He was wounded for our transgressions, He was bruised for our iniquities; the chastisement for our peace was upon Him, and by His stripes we are healed."

Jesus bore our grief, and even though grief is a normal response to trials, we do not have to carry it alone. He already bore it. The suffering Jesus endured for our healing was also for the healing of our emotions.

In God's abundant mercy He gave us a living hope through the resurrection of Jesus Christ. We read in 1 Peter, "In this you greatly rejoice, though now for a little while, if need be, you have been grieved by various trials, that the genuineness of your faith, being much more precious than gold that perishes, though it is tested by fire, may be found to praise, honor, and glory at the revelation of Jesus Christ, whom having not seen you love" (1 Pet. 1:6–8).

Sometimes your faith is tested by fire, but your trials can ultimately bring praise, honor, and glory to our Lord and Savior Jesus Christ. Cast all your cares upon Him, for He cares for you.

Chapter 7

THE DARKNESS OF DEPRESSION

DEPRESSION WAS A serious problem for me after the accident. The enemy pounced on me and tormented me over my decision to take the shortcut home that night. At times the depression was so severe that it was difficult or impossible for me to function and carry out routine daily tasks. I began to lose hope and literally thought I was losing my mind.

People who have suffered with severe depression say that it feels as though they have fallen from daylight into a black hole where they are stuck with no way out. Severe depression does not pass easily. It's not the same as temporary moodiness or disappointment over losing the national championship game.

Severe and lasting depression—clinically known as major depressive disorder—affects approximately 14.8 million American adults in any given year.[1] The number of people being diagnosed with depression is growing at an alarming rate—by approximately 20 percent each year. Adults suffering from depression are more likely than their nondepressed counterparts to be unemployed or recently divorced.[2]

According to the Centers for Disease Control and Prevention, depression can also adversely affect chronic conditions such as arthritis, asthma, cancer, and diabetes. From an employment stand-point, depressed people are more likely to experience absenteeism, decreased productivity, or short-term disability.[3]

Women report being depressed more often than men, but that seems to be because men don't want to admit they are depressed. However, severe depression is thought to be a major cause of suicide, and the suicide rate is significantly higher for men than for women.[4]

Depression is not just an American problem. Statistics indicate that 121 million people around the world are affected by depression, which causes 850,000 suicides every year. It might be surprising to learn those in the high-income countries—especially France, the Netherlands, and the United States—report a higher incidence of depression. The exception is India, where major depression is reported by nearly 36 percent of the population. Cross-culturally women are twice as likely as men to suffer from depression if they lose a partner, whether from death, divorce, or separation.[5]

THREE LEVELS OF DEPRESSION

Lisa Rathbun, a licensed clinical social worker who frequently counsels those dealing with depression, describes three levels of depression: low-grade, middle-range or moderate, and severe.[6] Symptoms of low-grade depression include feeling that things should be more fun than they are. A sense of a dark cloud overhead dulls feelings, and the person might seem empty or numb. People with low-grade depression still function and can be social, so their depression can go unnoticed. When symptoms of low-grade depression are present, the person might not be aware of the impact depression may be having on his or her stress levels, decision making, or self-perception.

Middle- or moderate-level depression might bring an increase in irritability and/or frustration as well as emotional outbursts. The opposite can be seen as well. The person might shut down, experience low energy or enjoyment, and be easily overwhelmed and stressed. The individual will develop a negative outlook or focus on life events.

This is the kind of depression I faced. I felt like I was in a hole because I was listening to so many lies from the enemy. I kept thinking the accident was my fault, and my thoughts were becoming toxic. I didn't stay in bed all day; I went about my daily routines. But I was miserable, hurt, and unhappy. I would go to minister, but I'd often wonder, "Why am I doing this?"

Severe depression involves significant shutdown and suicidal thoughts or focus. A severely depressed person is persistently hopeless and nonfunctioning. Once someone has become severely depressed, the person loses energy, motivation, the ability to make decisions, and even the desire to live. His self-esteem suffers, and his mind fills with reminders of all his failures in life—even those dating back to childhood. A severely depressed person will sleep too little or too much, eat too little or too much, feel tired constantly, and will experience aches and pains that cause him to worry about his health. Simply put, life is miserable and there seems to be no way to escape.

The factors that cause depression can be medical, biological, psychological, or spiritual in origin. In the field of clinical therapy, depression might fall under diagnostic terms such as bipolar disorder, postpartum depression, seasonal affective disorder, substance-induced mood disorder, and so on.

Sometimes medical conditions such as brain tumors, brain injuries, certain cancers, dementia, strokes, thyroid problems, and vitamin deficiencies can cause depression. A medical doctor can diagnose and sometimes treat depression that has biological or medical origins.

BRAIN CHEMISTRY AND DEPRESSION

According to Rathbun, "Chronic stress, even during childhood, alters brain chemistry. The three primary brain chemicals are serotonin, norepinephrine, and dopamine. Biochemical depression responds to medication. Situational depression does not, unless there was an underlying depression before the life event."[7]

One doctor who pioneered the diagnosis and treatment of certain brain-related disorders, including certain forms of depression, is Dr. Daniel Amen, a clinical neuroscientist, psychiatrist, and brain imaging expert. Through the use of brain imaging technology it is possible to determine if someone's brain is underfunctioning or overfunctioning in certain areas.[8] Once the brain scan pinpoints these areas of the brain, specialists can then help people find ways to optimize their brain function. Sometimes it takes nothing more than certain forms of exercise, proper nutrition and supplements, and a change in the way the person thinks.

According to Dr. Amen and other neuroscientists, one of the biggest buffers against emotional trauma is a healthy brain. If the brain works effectively, all other coping mechanisms tend to properly engage. When the brain is releasing the correct amount of chemicals such as dopamine, we can still experience joy in the midst of trouble.[9]

Wearing out the deep limbic area of the brain through drug abuse or repetitive behaviors such as Internet gambling, viewing pornography, playing video games, and even excessive e-mailing and texting will deplete us of dopamine, which then depletes us of joy and causes us to constantly need some kind of excitement. People then repeat the behaviors that released the dopamine, and addiction results. When drugs and addictive behaviors deplete the brain's dopamine, it means there is little of the chemical left when the time comes to perform meaningful activities such as working a job or completing homework.[10]

Some of the suggested ways to keep the brain healthy are to curb the use of all stimulants, exercise, laugh, engage in meaningful activities (such as volunteering), develop an attitude of appreciation and gratitude, and find enjoyment and meaning in the little things in life.[11]

Abraham Lincoln experienced depressive tendencies that could have been caused by a brain injury when he was twelve years old, or depression might have been inherited from his mother, whom Lincoln described as having "eyes as pools of sadness." Lincoln used humor to brighten his mood. He was so tense on election night in 1864 that he read a book of humor to calm his nerves, which caused people to think he was not taking the presidential election seriously.[12]

Today doctors know that laughter is healing. A hearty laugh enhances the immune system, lowers blood pressure, increases oxygen levels, and triggers endorphins in the brain, which can decrease pain and bring about feelings of euphoria. Laughter soothes tension, stimulates circulation, and relaxes muscles, all of which help reduce some of the physical symptoms of stress.[13]

There is no question that laughter improves your mood and helps lessen depression and anxiety. Even the Bible tells us that "a merry heart does good like a medicine, but a broken spirit dries the bones" (Prov. 17:22, MEV). "A merry heart makes a cheerful countenance, but by sorrow of the heart the spirit is broken" (Prov. 15:13, MEV).

THOUGHTS AND WORDS

Modern medicine is proving that the Bible is correct. Dr. Caroline Leaf, author of *Who Switched off My Brain*, also writes about how damaging toxic thoughts, emotions, words, choices, and dreams can be to your health. A massive body of research collectively shows that up to 80 percent of physical, emotional, and mental health issues today could be a direct result of our thought lives.[14]

At one time the scientific community did not believe thoughts had an effect on the body. When no medical cause was found for an illness, the patient was often told, "It's all in your head." This generally meant that the patient was imagining the symptoms. Now we know that "all in your head" could mean that you need to change your thought life!

Philippians 4:8 tells us that whatever things are true, whatever things are noble, whatever things are just, whatever things are pure, whatever things are lovely, whatever things are of good report, if there is any virtue and if there is anything praiseworthy, we are to meditate on these things.

We are told in 2 Corinthians 10:5 to cast down arguments and every high thing that exalts itself against the knowledge of God, and to bring every thought into captivity to the obedience of Christ. Proverbs 23:7 tells us that as a man thinks in his heart, so is he.

Our thoughts matter because fear and stress can cause depression. Short-term stress is not necessarily a bad thing, but stress becomes a problem when it moves from a temporary position in your life to a permanent position and causes fear. Negative, fear-driven thoughts trigger more than fourteen hundred known physical and chemical responses, which activate more than thirty different hormones and neurotransmitters that can throw the body into a frantic state.[15]

A believer should never suffer depression due to fear, because fear is not from God. The Bible tells us:

> For God has not given us a spirit of fear, but of power and of love and of a sound mind.
> —2 TIMOTHY 1:7

> Do not fear, for I am with you; do not be dismayed, for I am your God. I will strengthen you, I will help you, yes, I will uphold you with My righteous right hand.
> —ISAIAH 41:10, MEV

> I sought the LORD, and He answered me, and delivered me from all my fears.
> —PSALM 34:4, MEV

> For you did not receive the spirit of bondage again to fear, but you received the Spirit of adoption by whom we cry out, "Abba, Father."
> —ROMANS 8:15

These are some of the verses I quoted again and again when I was overcoming my fear of driving. I couldn't just speak them once or twice; I had to repeatedly remind myself of God's Word in order to break the hold fear had on me.

Medically speaking, every thought, whether positive or negative, goes through the same electrical and chemical cycle when it forms. As the thoughts grow and become permanent, branches (called dendrites) form and connections become stronger. The medical community now understands that if we change our thinking, some of those branches go away and new ones form.[16]

These branches network with other thoughts, thus giving the brain the capacity to rewire itself, for good or bad, depending on your thoughts. When your thoughts begin to line up positively with the Word of God and the brain rewires itself to overcome a lifetime of wrong thinking, Dr. Leaf says, "Spiritually, this is renewing the mind."[17]

Biblically speaking, Romans 12:2 tells us, "Do not be conformed to this world, but be transformed by the renewing of your mind, that you may prove what is the good and acceptable and perfect will of God" (MEV). According to W. E. Vine, the renewing of the mind means "the adjustment of the moral and spiritual vision and thinking to the mind of God which is designed to have a transforming effect upon the life."[18] To renew your mind means that your thoughts are under the controlling power of the indwelling of the Holy Spirit. Notice how this requires the willing response of the believer.

Bible teacher Rick Renner made a simple but powerful observation when he wrote, "Satan knows that empty heads are much easier to deceive. That's why he loves it when he finds a believer who has made no effort to fill his mind with truth from God's Word. The devil knows he has found another empty head just waiting for him to come along and fill it—and he's happy to oblige. Who or what is going to control your mind? God and His Word, or the enemy and his lies?"[19]

It is vital that we continually keep our minds renewed with the Word of God, because depression often hits in those times when we feel helpless and hopeless. When terrible things happen over and over and there seems to be no way out, a person can begin to believe that life has dealt them a bad card and things will always be this way. Even the Bible tells us in Proverbs 13:12 that hope deferred (delayed) makes the heart sick, but fulfilled desire is a tree of life. Adam Clarke's commentary says:

> Hope deferred maketh the heart sick—When once a good is discovered, want of it felt, strong desire for the possession excited, and the promise of attainment made on grounds unsuspected, so that the reality of the thing and the certainty of the promise are manifest, hope posts forward to realize the blessing. Delay in the gratification pains the mind; the increase of the delay prostrates and sickens the heart; and if delay sickens the heart, ultimate disappointment kills it. But when the thing desired, hoped for, and expected comes, it is a tree of life, חיים עץ *ets chaiyim, the tree of lives:* it comforts and invigorates both body and soul.[20]

When hope is delayed, the soul becomes wounded, grieved, and even sick. The delay leads to disappointment; disappointment begins to kill hope; and before long, negative thoughts take over the mind and negative words flow from the mouth. It can become a vicious cycle.

Depressed people think extremely negative thoughts. Doctors once believed that depression caused negative thinking, but they later began to suggest that it was the negative thinking that caused depression. The Bible supports that position. People can think and speak negatively about themselves or hear negative comments so often that they begin to believe those things. If your mind is bombarded with thoughts such as, "You are worthless, ugly, and will never amount to anything," before long you come into agreement with those words and you may even change your brain chemistry. Negative beliefs brought about by negative thoughts and words are discouraging and bring defeat to our lives.

After the accident I felt worthless and so guilty. I thought, "Here I am alive and my family's dead." I thought my ministry was over, but as time went on— and we're talking a lot of time—I began to realize that my thinking was wrong. I remembered that God's Word says in Jeremiah 29:11 that I do have hope and a future, and it's the devil who says I don't. It's the devil who was saying I can't overcome, because God says He *always* causes me to triumph (2 Cor. 2:14). I had been listening to what the devil said first—that I was guilty of causing the accident, that my ministry was over, that I couldn't help anybody. But when I made a conscious choice to start listening to what God's Word says, my thoughts started to change.

I meditated on verses such as the following:

> But You, O LORD, are a shield for me, my glory
> and the One who raises up my head.
> —PSALM 3:3, MEV

> Out of Zion, the perfection of beauty, God has
> shined. Our God will come, and will not keep
> silent.
> —PSALM 50:2–3, MEV

He shepherded them according to the integrity
of his heart and guided them by the skillfulness
of his hands.

—PSALM 78:72, MEV

In all these things we are more than conquerors
through Him who loved us. For I am persuaded
that neither death nor life, neither angels nor
principalities nor powers, neither things present
nor things to come, neither height nor depth,
nor any other created thing, shall be able to
separate us from the love of God, which is in
Christ Jesus our Lord.

—ROMANS 8:37–39, MEV

I had to choose to start listening to the right voice,
and I had to keep believing that voice when I didn't
"feel" anything. When there was no church service and I didn't feel an ounce of God, I had to keep
believing that God's Word is true and that God is for
me and not against me. I had to remind myself, "I will
not be defeated in this because I will not quit trying."
And faith began to rise. I began to call those things as
though they already were—hope, peace, fruitfulness
in ministry—and I began to rejoice in the Lord. Not
every day. Some days went great, and some days felt
like the bottom fell out. Some days I'd say to Janet,
"Pray for me. I'm really battling this today." There were
times when the negative thoughts came so hard and
so fast that I felt like my mind was going to shut down.

But I kept coming back to God. I said, "God, You've
got to destroy the traumatic effects of the unexpected
attacks on my life." I had to activate my faith. What
happened to me was worse than my worst nightmare.

But faith never loses a battle. So I took that faith as a weapon and began to use it against the enemy, and God began to heal me. I can't say when the healing came, because it happened over time. But healing came.

I can say without hesitation that if one does not choose to think differently, the negative thoughts that lead to depression will take you down. They can cause you to lose your life. I know firsthand that God is a restorer. When I began to believe His Word instead of the enemy's lies, He restored to me the hope, joy, and peace the enemy tried to steal.

Dealing With Life Traumas

Traumatic events that occur throughout our lives can be devastating, and both emotions and brain chemistry can be affected. Physical abuse, verbal abuse, rejection, and other traumas create stress, and severe stress strains the body's systems—including the brain. If you react to these traumas with fear, anxiety, bitterness, and unforgiveness, certain chemicals will be released that have a dreadful, long-term effect on the body.

Dr. Caroline Leaf writes that stress chemicals don't know when they have overstayed their welcome, and they will bury themselves deep inside your mind and become part of you, building up like a volcano and erupting in anger, hostility, and resentment. Since emotions cause real physiological reactions, they can cause both mental and physical illness. Even cancer can be caused by these stress chemicals, because it is a properly functioning immune system that kills most cancer cells.[21]

Let's look at the biblical instructions in Philippians 4:4–8: "Rejoice in the Lord always. Again I will say, rejoice! Let everyone come to know your gentleness. The Lord is at hand. Be anxious for nothing, but in everything, by prayer and supplication with gratitude, make your requests known to God. And the peace of God, which surpasses all understanding, will protect your hearts and minds through Christ Jesus. Finally, brothers, whatever things are true, whatever things are honest, whatever things are just, whatever things are pure, whatever things are lovely, whatever things are of good report, if there is any virtue, and if there is any praise, think on these things" (MEV).

Here we are told to rejoice, be thankful, and think on things that are noble, pure, and of good report. By this we will have the peace of God that surpasses all understanding, and God will guard our hearts and minds through Christ.

The stress of traumatic events throughout our lives can cause hidden anger, bitterness, unforgiveness, depression, and a host of physical and emotional problems. An unbiblical response to traumatic events can also open the door for the enemy to torment, attack, and oppress us. Medical providers will generally treat severe depression by trying to "fix" the problem with antidepressants. But antidepressants do not get to the root of the problem caused by the trauma. These are the kinds of situations that have spiritual solutions, and God is able to both heal and deliver us from the stronghold of depression brought about through traumatic life events.

Consider Sarah's story. Sarah is a born-again, Spirit-filled believer whose problems began in childhood, but it took decades before she found herself dealing with severe depression resulting from these early events and not knowing what to do or where to turn.

Before Sarah was conceived, her mother was told that she could never have another child. But she conceived and experienced severe hemorrhaging five months into the pregnancy. Doctors said she would die if they did not take the baby. Indeed, she lost so much blood that she died.

Sarah's mother was not born again and did not attend church, though she knew about Jesus because her parents were Baptist. When she died, she entered a tunnel and saw someone who she thought must be Jesus. Knowing that she was dying, she made this promise: "If You will let me and the baby live, I promise I will give this baby to You."

She came back to life, and the hemorrhaging stopped. Two months later Sarah was born prematurely. She almost died that day, but miraculously she survived.

Sarah's dad served two tours in Vietnam, and when he returned home the second time, he left Sarah's mother for another woman. Sarah recalls:

> Mom sat in the living room for a year, depressed, with the curtains drawn, chain smoking cigarettes the whole time. I was about the only person she talked to.
>
> Later my mother became involved in areas of the occult—horoscopes, fortune-telling, and such. Our home was filled with Japanese idols that she purchased while stationed there in the army with her first husband. Her second

husband, my dad, was a Freemason. There was a lot of alcohol and drug abuse in our home, and the people around me seemed to always be in trouble. My mother told me that I was ugly and that I wasn't wanted, which caused me to have a bad self-image. So this gives you an idea of the foundation that was being laid for me.

To make matters worse, when I was eight years old, I was molested. Then at age twenty-one I was raped. When the enemy has an assignment against someone's life, he will do everything to keep that person from fulfilling his or her God-given destiny. I had never been involved in promiscuous behavior, drugs, or alcohol, and it was a miracle that God protected me from all that in the midst of a dysfunctional atmosphere at home.

When I was ten years of age, my mother allowed me to attend church by riding the church bus. She even purchased a children's Bible for me from a salesman who sold them door-to-door. I read that entire Bible, and my heroine was Deborah. I craved the kind of intimacy she had with God.

Even though I was smart, having been high school valedictorian and winning a scholarship to college, I never seemed to excel. Since my divorced mother made minimum wage, I worked after school to help her. My bachelor's degree is in biblical studies, and I attended graduate school for counseling. But after one year I got married and dropped out of school to support my husband while he finished graduate school. He obtained his degree, but the marriage did not last, and my life continued to be one struggle after another. I moved to another part of the state and eventually lost my job and then wrecked my car in an accident. Jobless and without a car, I felt like I had hit rock bottom.

I tried to get in touch with my dad, but it was impossible to connect with him because of his girlfriend. I moved once again and started at the very bottom at minimum wage. After a few years I was promoted, and things seemed to be going well. I always had a close and intimate walk with the Lord, and I treasured that. I could simply say, "Lord, I want to be in Your presence," and I could enter the secret place anytime I asked.

Then one day the Lord showed me a black tornado and told me that this was going to hit me at my job. I knew changes were coming, but I had dealt with this kind of thing before and thought I could handle it.

Management changes did occur at work, and about two months after the Lord showed me the tornado, the depression hit. I felt like I was in a dark pit. It was as though one day I had a close walk with God, and the next day the umbilical cord that connected me to Him had been cut. Up to that point I could hear His voice, and we were very close. But when this depression hit me, it was like a Gethsemane experience where I was saying, "Lord, why have You forsaken me?"

This depression lasted months, and the months turned into two and a half years. I experienced agony in my spirit and soul. I lost interest in everything, having no desire to go on. I felt like a living dead person—dead except for the emotional pain I experienced. When I was alone, I wept constantly. I didn't want to eat. I felt like I was dealing with oppression from the enemy. A doctor wanted to prescribe antidepressants, but I saw what drugs had done to my family and I wanted no part of that.

I still attended church, still loved the Lord, and had asked a few people to pray for me. Friends prayed for me and loved me, but nothing helped. I was not suicidal, but every day I prayed for God to let me die. I felt like my connection to Him was gone, and I could not sense His presence at all. It was agony. My spirit was crushed.

One night I was praying at church with a friend from Africa. As we left the prayer service, she asked me how I was doing. Once she realized how badly I needed help, she contacted her pastor in Africa and asked him to pray for me. He took this task so seriously that he prayed and fasted an entire week, even turning his church over to his assistant during that time. After the fast my friend and I connected with this pastor on a three-way call. He prayed a prayer of deliverance over me, breaking the satanic assignments that were hindering my life. A month later we connected once more by phone, and he prayed for me again.

The three of us e-mailed back and forth, and he wrote things such as, "As I was praying for you, God said He wants you to abide by His name, Faithful and True. Spend time in His presence and in prayer, and declare your total dependence on Him. You are a treasured vessel and God will make you whole. He loves you and is working a consecration for a higher calling, a calling before you were conceived in your mother's womb."

Then he invited me to come to Africa to be a guest in his family's home. I never thought I would go to Africa alone, but I did. The pastor and his family were extremely hospitable, even building a special room onto their home for me to stay in while I was there. I was the first white person to ever visit their home or their church. In fact, I was about the only white person I saw while I was there. The family treated me like royalty during the three weeks that I was there, and they went to great lengths to help me.

Every morning we arose early and prayed. Pastor waited for the Holy Spirit to tell him how to pray for me. The first time he prayed, he was making hand motions as though he was cutting roots, which were the roots of early problems such as rejection. He prayed for the Lord to breathe resurrection life back into me and to pour His oil (representing healing) and His wine (representing joy) into me. Another time he prayed against any satanic altars related to the occult activity of my parents and previous generations.

There are altars of God and there are satanic altars that are raised against children of God to keep them from fulfilling the purpose of God in their lives. This is where evil is programmed against God's children and where demonic spirits are assigned to fight against us. Just as God has covenants, the enemy also attempts to seal contracts against us, and permission is given by the evil things in which you or previous generations of your family have been involved. The more wickedness you or your family engage in, the more power the enemy has to wreck your life.

When the pastor prayed for me, he informed the enemy that he had no power over me and that the evil forces that had been working against me were forbidden to return.

One time the pastor was praying for the Lord to heal the deep hurt, grief, and disappointments in my life. The hurt that I felt during that prayer was so deep that I could only make a moaning sound. God shows me things visually, and during the time that the pastor was praying, the Lord allowed me to see that He was transferring my pain to the pastor, who then gave it to the Lord on my behalf. I asked the pastor afterward if the Lord transferred my pain to him, and at first he did not want to answer. But I kept questioning him, and finally he said yes.

The best image I can give of this is the picture of Jesus bearing our grief, sorrow, and sins and taking them to the cross on our behalf. Jesus bore the sorrows of people who had not even been born yet. Galatians 6:2 tells us to carry one another's burdens, and in this way we fulfill the law of Christ.

After that occurred, I noticed that I did not feel the same pain and depression anymore. Once in a while I feel pain again, but I know that I must keep claiming and walking in my deliverance. Righteousness, peace, and joy are our heritage as children of God.

Since receiving help from this pastor, I no longer feel as though I am in a black hole. I feel different spiritually. It is almost as though I am going through another spiritual rebirth—the building of a stronger foundation.

I believe the reason the Lord had to send me to Africa is because there are not many people in the United States who understand how to deliver Christians from this kind of thing. But in Africa the pastors deal with this often, and they understand what is necessary to help someone overcome the oppression, bondage, and strongholds of the enemy that try to destroy people's lives, even those who are Spirit-filled.

During this time of depression God gave me a picture of a garden. The garden gate was closed, and angels were inside digging up the garden's foundation. They were digging up every trace of a bad foundation, anything that could be a problem the enemy could use to defeat me. But God was not in that garden with the angels; instead, He was outside the closed gate, watching as the work was done.

The understanding I received was that God was supervising the work of removing the bad foundations in my life and rebuilding them properly and on solid, biblical ground. When you have this kind of rebuilt foundation, the enemy cannot infiltrate.

I had been a sponge for whatever the enemy wanted to do in my life because of my family's ungodly foundation of occult activity, alcohol, drugs, molestation, and negative belief systems. I had to be delivered from strongholds related to rejection and abandonment by my dad, generational curses, ungodly soul ties, word curses, and life traumas. Biblically I thought I understood how all of these things work. But now I see that God has to peel away these things like the layers of an onion, and sometimes it takes awhile for us to deal with all of these issues and past traumas.

Recently the Lord gave me these verses in 1 Peter 4:12–13 to explain what I was going through: "Beloved, do not think it strange concerning the fiery trial which is to try you, as though some strange thing happened to you; but rejoice to the extent that you partake of Christ's sufferings, that when His glory is revealed, you may also be glad with exceeding joy." I understood that the test would have a purpose, and it would not last forever.

Like a potter creating something from clay, God had to take me off the wheel and remold me. Thanks to Him and the help of an African pastor, I now know that the Lord will perfect the work He started. I am fearfully and wonderfully made and created in the image and likeness of God. He will turn my ashes into beauty.

THE ROOT OF THE PROBLEM

It is a tragic fact of life that, intentionally or unintentionally, people do terrible things, both to themselves and others. A drunkard gets behind the wheel of a car and drives. Couples verbally and physically abuse each other and their own children. Pedophiles molest children. Drug addicts rob and murder to feed their habit. Terrorists kill innocent people. Think of all the wicked world leaders who have been responsible for the deaths of millions of people throughout history. When people live in sin, they engage in all sorts of activities they would never consider if they were living a repentant and righteous life before God. And society suffers because of it.

Wrong acts committed by other people cause a host of problems for the victims. Children carry the scars into adulthood, and the root of the problem must be dealt with if we are to live the abundant life Jesus promised. We can be saved and Spirit-filled, but that does not mean we are free from the consequences of problems we neither asked for nor caused.

The blame for this oppression belongs with the adversary, known in Scripture as the thief, murderer, and annihilator. Jesus is the Good Shepherd who came to give us abundant life. We read in John 10:9–11: "I am the door. If anyone enters through Me, he will be saved and will go in and out and find pasture. The thief does not come, except to steal and kill and destroy. I came that they may have life, and that they may have it more abundantly. I am the good shepherd. The good shepherd lays down His life for the sheep" (MEV).

THE ADVERSARY'S ATTACKS

Satan tempts, steals joy and peace, robs people of a productive life, and attacks when we are weak and vulnerable. He even tried to tempt Jesus after a forty-day fast by suggesting that He turn stones into bread so He would have something to satisfy His hunger. Jesus responded in Matthew 4:4 by quoting the Word: "It is written, 'Man shall not live by bread alone, but by every word that proceeds out of the mouth of God'" (MEV)

Look at Elijah. We read in 1 Kings 18 that Jezebel

had been killing the prophets of God, and those who were still alive all seemed to be hiding in caves. But Elijah bravely confronted Jezebel's husband, King Ahab, calling him a destroyer of Israel because he abandoned the Lord's commands and followed Baal.

Elijah called fire down on an altar that had been soaked with water after the prophets of Baal danced around the altar for several hours, cutting themselves with knives and spears as they tried to convince their god to light the fire before Elijah's God could perform the miraculous feat. When fire consumed Elijah's altar, it proved to the people that Baal was a false god and that the God of Abraham, Isaac, and Jacob was the one true God who reigned supreme.

After that, Elijah took Jezebel's prophets of Baal to the Brook Kishon and slaughtered all 450 of them. God performed another miracle and brought rain to end a severe drought that had lasted nearly three years.

When Jezebel learned what Elijah had done, she threatened to kill him. Elijah became fearful and immediately ran for his life, ending up a hundred miles away in Beersheba. Then he went another day's journey where, there in the wilderness, sitting under a juniper tree, Elijah prayed to die.

He had done everything God told him to do, and now Jezebel was going to kill him. What was wrong with Elijah? It most likely was not his fear of Jezebel. It is more likely he was simply worn out, discouraged, depressed, and hungry.

Elijah was certain that he was the only prophet of God still alive. But he rested, and the Lord sent angels to feed him and bring him water, and this gave him strength to walk forty days and nights to Mount Horeb. God also assured him that he was not alone; indeed, there were seven thousand in Israel who had not bowed to Baal. Just as God met Elijah at his point of need, He will meet us at ours.

Sin and Depression

There was a time when Christians assumed that depression always meant the afflicted person had sin in his or her life. Now we have enough knowledge to know that is not always the case. However, we must be aware that a lifestyle of sin and rebellion will lead to guilt, condemnation, and demonic oppression or possession, all of which can lead to depression. The only way to overcome that kind of depression is through repentance.

"Spiritually related depression will result in ineffective medication results," says clinical social worker Lisa Rathbun. "Some people are dealing with inhabiting [demonic] spirits that lead to depression symptoms. Sometimes these spirits attached themselves to the person at a very young age due to a traumatic event that occurred at that time. Unfortunately this area is all but completely overlooked in the traditional counseling realm. Even the majority of Christian counselors will not venture in this direction. And unfortunately most pastors are not discerning this in the people they counsel.

"The goal of the enemy is to distract people from God. Depression can keep someone from experiencing God's joy and presence, and the tormenting voice they hear convinces them that God is far away and uncaring of their pain. These spirits must be dealt with in order for the person to receive complete deliverance and healing."[22]

In instances where sin is the cause of depression, the solution is repentance. After confession of sins, repentance, and a turning away from a lifestyle of sin, God gives freedom from condemnation and guilt. Those sins you committed are forgiven and wiped away as though they never existed.

The church also has a responsibility to forgive and restore those who have sinned, and the apostle Paul told us why. In 2 Corinthians 2:5–11 he wrote about a man whose sin had caused a lot of people pain. But Paul advised the church that the man had suffered enough because of the punishment inflicted, and now he should be forgiven and comforted, lest he become overwhelmed by excessive grief. The church was told to reaffirm their love for this man, as this would be a test of their character and obedience. Paul ended with a final warning to forgive so that the people would not be taken advantage of by Satan.

One of the unfortunate consequences of a lifestyle of sin and rebellion is the unstable foundation people create for themselves and their children through their actions. Just as we saw with Sarah's example, the sinful lifestyle of parents can have generational consequences that give the enemy a legal right to attack.

Until we understand and identify the root cause of our problems, and then use the Word of God, the name of Jesus, the blood of Jesus, and the authority Jesus gave us to break those attacks of the enemy, people will suffer and fail to live the abundant life Jesus promised.

Idolatry and occult activity are particularly damaging. One of the Ten Commandments, found in Exodus 20:5–6, is a warning not to bow down to or serve other gods or images: "For I, the LORD your God, am a jealous God, visiting the iniquity of the fathers upon the children to the third and fourth generations of those who hate Me, but showing mercy to thousands, to those who love Me and keep My commandments."

Children and society in general pay a terrible price when people choose to live in sin, idolatry, and rebellion against God. Don't leave a legacy of trouble for your children and the generations to come.

SOLUTIONS FOR DEPRESSION

Since depression has many causes, it is impossible to develop the perfect cure for every case. If the depression is medical or biological in origin, then of course it should be treated by a qualified health care provider. There are other reasons for depression, though, and we should do everything possible to take practical steps to care for ourselves.

Through the story of Elijah we see biblically that hunger and fatigue can cause temporary feelings of depression, so the obvious solution is to rest and eat. Some of us are so deprived of sleep and good nutrition it is a miracle the depression statistics are not much higher. It is important to get just the right amount of sleep, which the medical community says is between seven and eight hours each night.

It is also helpful to get proper exercise. This generally means engaging in cardiovascular activity such as walking or anything aerobic, as medical studies seem to indicate this is the best kind of exercise to help depression. Proper nutrition is also important, so in addition to eating a balanced diet, consider adding nutritional supplements to help with any vitamin deficiency.

Regular exposure to sunlight is also known to help some forms of depression. People who live in northern environments that are dark during the winter often choose to spend time under special lights that mimic natural sunlight.

Another suggestion is to engage in a hobby that you enjoy. I have already mentioned that playing tennis with my family helped me. It is not important that you be an expert at whatever you choose; the important thing is to find something you enjoy and do it.

Do not stay in a dark room and focus on your troubles all day. Volunteer for a worthwhile activity. Even though severely depressed people might not feel up to doing volunteer work, it does provide a network of people who have a similar vision, and it takes your mind off your own circumstances and puts your own problems in proper perspective.

As a gospel singer and preacher, I was always on the platform. But as soon as I was done ministering, I'd find Janet and make a beeline for the car or my hotel. If I had it to do over again, I think I would have gotten involved in grief recovery programs and attended more church functions to stay connected to other believers. People can say the craziest things when you're grieving. I had a guy once tell me to just get over it. He meant well, but he really hurt me at the time. If someone said something like that to me, I shut him off. But being in fellowship with others, especially those who understand what you're going through, can aid in the healing process.

On the other hand, being around the wrong people can be harmful. If you have friends who are a bad influence in your life, tell them good-bye and cultivate some new friendships.

Certain kinds of music are also powerful. Consider what happened when David played the harp for King Saul after the Spirit of the Lord departed from Saul and a distressing spirit troubled him (1 Sam. 16:14–23). Saul became refreshed and well, and at the sound of the music the distressing spirit would depart from him.

There is also a spirit of heaviness, according to Isaiah 61:3. God will give beauty for ashes, the oil of joy for mourning, and the garment of praise for the spirit of heaviness. One of the ways to deal with the spirit of heaviness is to put on the garment of praise. To put on the garment of praise means to be wrapped up in praise. What is praise? It is thanksgiving; it is singing and speaking words that glorify and magnify God. Praise is showing appreciation for everything the Lord has done for you.

Do not neglect your spiritual life. Get involved in church and attend services regularly. Most health care providers will not suggest this, but studies have shown that faith plays an important role in the improvement of health and depression. Pray. Read the

Bible and quote the promises of God over your life. This will help renew your mind.[23]

Close every door that you have opened to the enemy, and repent for the sins you committed because of those open doors. Ask the Lord to heal your past hurts, even those as far back as childhood. Tell someone you can trust—preferably a believer who is a good listener who will also pray for you—that you are depressed. Most likely people can tell something is wrong, so you might as well admit it.

Do not make excuses for yourself or try to justify your depression. We all have a responsibility to deal with our behavior and live lives that are free from emotional bondage and spiritual strongholds. When you have a problem, admit that something needs to be done, and don't blame others for your behavior. Yes, other people might have a lot to do with it, but you will never overcome as long as you continue to blame someone else for why you are the way you are.

Stop asking why, why, why. Why did this happen? Why did God allow this? Yes, I spent plenty of time asking why. And had I continued to ask why, I might have wallowed in my sorrow and ended up with chronic, severe depression that would have destroyed my family, marriage, life, and ministry. Be thankful to God for all that He has done throughout your life, because no matter what you have gone through, things always could have been worse.

If you hold unforgiveness toward someone, forgive. We will talk more about forgiveness in a later chapter, but for now suffice it to say, do not hold grudges and do not live with bitterness. You can take a pharmacy

FORGIVING the **UNFORGIVABLE**

full of antidepressants, but if you are living with unforgiveness, you will never overcome your depression. Spiritual issues such as these must be dealt with. We must always remain spiritually vigilant.

When you are facing depression and find yourself overcome with thoughts of giving up, it is vital that you change the channel. Change from that depressing channel to the victory channel. Remind yourself of all the good things that have happened in your life. Remember the many things you have accomplished by the grace and help of God. Recall the times that God healed you or delivered you. Be thankful to Him for those things.

I had to start remembering and being thankful for all the good times I had with my family. After I did this for a while, my mental outlook improved and my strength returned. Change your thoughts and dwell on positive memories, and watch the depression gradually lift. Anytime you find yourself focused on the negative, change the channel and consider the good in your life.

I am so grateful to God for my wife, Janet. I talked with her a lot about the way I was feeling, how I was tormented with guilt for taking the shortcut that night—and for stopping to get something to eat in the first place. If Janet got tired of listening to me, she never let on. She would tell me, "Craig, you didn't know what would happen. You had no idea that taking a shortcut that night would end up the way it did. Had you have known, you never would have done it, right?" She helped me to see that the accident wasn't my fault.

Sometimes in my anger and pain I'd ask her

questions she couldn't answer: Why didn't God prevent the accident? Why didn't He miraculously save Dad and Grandmother Pauline? Each time she would tell me that she didn't have the answer, but God did. Sometimes I'd think, "Is that all you have to say?" But in the end it would push me back to my only true solution, the Lord. And I'd tell Him, "Lord, I keep blaming myself. You have to help me." And He did.

He'll do the same for you. Allow the Lord to help you deal with your problems. If your problem seems to have no known origin, ask the Lord to show you the root of your problem, and allow Him to dig up that root and rebuild your foundation. It might not be an easy process, but it will be worth it when the rebuilding is complete. Through your humility and submission He will turn your bad situation into life more abundant. Your testimony can then be used to help other people learn to overcome by the Word, the name and blood of Jesus, and the power of the Holy Spirit. Just as in the story of Joseph in Genesis 37, that which the enemy meant for evil, the Lord will turn around for good.

No matter what you are facing right now or might face in the future, God wants you to come through it victoriously. God has a plan for you, just as He does for me. In the midst of my depression and bitterness I thought that plan was destroyed. I thought I would never preach or sing again with any kind of effectiveness because I was hurt, confused, angry, depressed, and suicidal. I thought I had nothing to offer people anymore, and I thought the ministry God had given me had come to a screeching halt. But that was a lie of the enemy to keep me from doing the things God wanted me to do in this life.

I have compassion for people who are dealing with depression because I have been there. But I want to tell you, in the matchless name of Jesus, the name that is above every other name, to get up and move forward. You will see your situation change, and doors will open for new opportunities. Every day you will find yourself a little more healed.

Keep pressing, keep believing, keep praying, stay in the Word, and stay close to God. He will help you, deliver you, and set your feet back on the Rock. He will see you through. Of this I am living proof.

Chapter 8

AN IRREVERSIBLE DECISION

DURING THE TIME I suffered from severe depression, I also battled thoughts of suicide, even though I knew suicide was wrong. I knew what the Bible says about the value of life and that one of the Ten Commandments tells us not to kill. But I was trying to deal with my pain.

People who feel depressed, hopeless, helpless, and overwhelmed with their circumstances often see no way out except to end their life. That's what happened to me. For a time I saw no way out of the pain I was experiencing. Ministry, family—nothing seemed to soothe the intense grief I was feeling. I never went so far as to pull out a gun or buy some pills, but I would sometimes think, "You need to end your life. Then it will be over."

Somehow—and I know it was the Lord—I was able to see that was wrong thinking, and I'd actually say out loud, "Devil, get behind me. That's a lie from hell. I don't receive that!" But the thoughts would come again and again. I can't count the number of times I had to fight off the enemy's attacks. I would remind myself of what Paul Walker said, "I will not be defeated because I will not quit." But still there were days when I didn't think I'd make it through. I remember once going to my cousin and asking him to pray for me. I didn't go into detail, but he prayed for me and he rebuked suicidal thoughts, and they left. After that, I started to get better. The thoughts returned a few times, but I'd fill my mind with God's Word, and the Lord would always bring me through until the thoughts stopped coming altogether.

Suicide is a major, preventable problem. In 2010 suicide was the tenth leading cause of death in the United States, accounting for more than thirty-eight thousand deaths.[1] The overall rate was 12.4 suicide deaths per one hundred thousand people.[2] An estimated twenty-five suicide attempts occur for every one person who succeeds in committing suicide.[3]

Risk factors for suicide include depression or other mental disorders or a substance abuse disorder (often in combination with other mental disorders). Other risk factors include a prior suicide attempt, a family history of suicide, family violence, physical or sexual abuse, and exposure to others' suicidal behavior—family members, peers, or media figures.[4]

Depressed people also have a higher risk of attempted suicide when they mix suicidal thoughts with drugs or alcohol. Even certain prescription drugs used to treat depression list "thoughts of suicide" as one of the potential side effects. Drugs and alcohol, when used together, increase the potency of each other. So one alcoholic beverage and one dose of a drug could together equal the effect of multiple drinks and drug dosages. The end result is that thinking and short-term memory are impaired, so the chances of dying are greatly increased. People do things while intoxicated by drugs or alcohol that they might never do otherwise.

Suicide and suicidal behaviors are not normal responses to stress. Many people who deal with stressful situations have these risk factors, but they are not suicidal. Research shows that risk for suicide can be associated with changes in the brain's neurotransmitters, including serotonin levels. Decreased levels of serotonin have been found in the brains of people with depression, impulsive disorders, and a history of suicide attempts.[5]

People over age sixty-five have a disproportionately higher suicide rate,[6] and white males age eighty-five and older consistently have the highest suicide rate of any other age group.[7] Certain ethnic groups also have a higher risk of suicide. The lowest rates are among Hispanics, non-Hispanic blacks, and Asian and Pacific Islanders. The highest rates are among non-Hispanic whites, Alaska natives, and American Indians.

Among youth between the ages of ten and twenty-four suicide is a serious public health problem that results in the loss of around 4,600 lives each year. Suicide is the third leading cause of death in this age group. More attempt suicide than succeed, and each year approximately 157,000 youth receive emergency medical care for self-inflicted injuries.[8]

During the years 2005 to 2009 the highest suicide rates for those ages ten to twenty-four were among American Indian and Alaska natives.[9]

NATIVE AMERICAN YOUTH

Johnny Hughes, executive director of Indian Ministries of North America (IMNA), became aware of the problem with suicides among young Native Americans when he was visiting the Navajo reservation in New Mexico. He says, "An eight-year-old boy hung himself and left a note saying life was not worth living. One girl came to our teen camp on the Navajo reservation and was having a hard time dealing with some issues. When we got to the bottom of it, we found that her nine-year-old brother had hung himself. He had watched a movie that showed a scene where somebody hung himself, and the next day he was found hanging from a tree in his grandmother's yard. This could have been a copycat suicide, because the boy had a bad habit of emulating things he saw in movies. We soon realized that suicide on the reservations was a serious problem."[10]

Johnny said he realized the scope of this problem when a state of emergency was issued at the Pine Ridge Reservation in South Dakota. Teen suicide had become epidemic, and the elders and tribal leaders had tried all kinds of things, including suicide prevention programs. They tried taking the youth back to their traditional Native American roots, thinking that perhaps this was happening because the teens had gone too far toward the ways of the white man. But nothing worked.

Some of the Christian leaders on the reservation approached the elders and tribal leaders and asked if they could help. By this time the situation had gotten so far out of hand that the tribal leaders were willing to let the Christians try to do something.

Indian Ministries of North America took a group of young people to Pine Ridge Reservation during one of their summer programs. That year over fifteen hundred young people under age twenty-five had attempted suicide. The fastest growing age for suicide attempts is age ten to fourteen. Johnny said, "When we contacted a suicide prevention agency on the reservation and told them we were coming, the agency told us not to come because they did not need us, our God, or our Bible. But we were already on our way, so we showed up anyway.

"The week leading up to our arrival there were five suicides. One nineteen-year-old girl had recently given birth to a baby, and she hung herself from a tree. In one month in this area there were twelve suicides. Later we learned that, according to a report, 150 teens on this reservation had gotten together and made a pact to commit suicide on the same night. Thankfully this was stopped in time. Suicide is now the second leading cause of death of people twenty-five years of age and younger on the reservations.

"The first thing we did when our youth group arrived at the Pine Ridge Reservation that summer was sing at the funeral of a twelve-year-old boy who went into his grandmother's basement and hung himself. What shocked me most about this funeral was the lack of emotion of the family and friends who were present at the funeral. When I asked why the people were so emotionless, I was told it was because most people expected their children to commit suicide. It wasn't a matter of if it would happen, but when. It had become so common that they had even created a slang term for it. Instead of calling it suicide, they called it 'going sideways.' Somebody who killed themselves 'went sideways.'"[11]

As heavy-hearted as the group was as they ministered to the families at Pine Ridge, they started receiving phone calls from their own reservations that a rash of suicides had begun to happen in their own neighborhoods on the Navajo reservations. The youth ministering with Johnny started calling home and finding out that their own cousins had committed suicide.

When Johnny prayed and asked the Lord why the enemy was targeting the Native American youth so heavily, he was reminded of the many prophetic words that have been spoken about an end-time revival among the Native Americans that will begin with the young people. The enemy knows this revival is coming, and he wants to take out as many young people as possible by killing the seed of this revival before it has a chance to take root and grow.

One summer six of the young people in the IMNA group tried to commit suicide. Johnny says, "We were on our way to pick up one girl, and I knew she was supposed to come on this trip because she was the first person the Lord showed me. When we called to say we were on our way, she replied that she could not go. We texted back and forth, and she said that she was seeing demonic beings and shadows roaming throughout her room, and they were tormenting her. She said, 'I cannot go because I cannot handle this anymore.' After a couple of hours of texting back and forth, the messages stopped.

"Two hours later we received a text telling us that she was going and things were better. We had no idea what happened to her until she gave her testimony at a church in Atlanta. During the two hours when we had no contact with her, she had tied an electrical cord around her neck and jumped off a chair in her closet. As she was gasping for her last breath, it was as though somebody cut the cord and she fell. She was on the floor for those two hours, and when she regained consciousness, there was an overwhelming presence of God in the room. The Lord spoke to her and said, 'You can't end it this way. I have a purpose for your life.'

"We sat down with her one day to attempt to get to the root of the problem. We always assumed it was hopelessness, and a lot of it is. Many of these young people on the reservations are born into and grow up in families of alcoholics who stay drunk all the time. At six years of age they get up in the morning for school and find a houseful of alcoholics passed out in their living room. The children go through the room and drink whatever is left of the alcohol. By the time these children are teenagers, they are already alcoholics.

"Many of these children see this lifestyle every day and wonder, 'Is this all there is to life?' They are beyond hopeless. These young people simply have no sense of self-worth and no sense of value.

"One of the telltale signs we recognized that led to suicide was that, in elementary school, children start erasing their skin with a pencil eraser until they burn off their skin and leave scars on their body. Then they advance to razor blades and begin to cut themselves. When we asked why they do this, they said it is because the pain is concentrated in one spot. All the pain they feel from everything around them dissipates as the pain is felt only on the spot where they cut themselves. They feel a kind of release.

"From burning themselves with erasers to cutting, the young people move to attempted suicide. Some try pills, while the older guys will shoot themselves. But the preferred method seems to be hanging.

"When young people have no self-worth and think they will never amount to anything and will always be like their parents, the likelihood increases that they will attempt suicide. Sometimes the parents will even perpetuate this. If they see that their child is attempting to better himself, they will say things such as, 'What makes you think you're better than we are?' They don't want their children to better themselves, forsake their identity and heritage, and move away from the reservation.

"About 40 percent of Native Americans still live on the reservation. Some leave and go to the big cities, but often they are unprepared to survive in this kind of environment, so they end up homeless and living on the streets. This leaves them in worse condition than they were in when they lived on the reservation, and they have no family in the city to help them."[12]

In Tennessee a woman went to her church to

work one Saturday and found a man lying in the doorway of the church. He was from the Pine Ridge Indian Reservation in South Dakota. He had been in Tennessee years earlier and was given someone's business card. When his circumstances seemed to be more than he could handle on the reservation, he bought a one-way bus ticket to Tennessee. He knew not a soul and had no driver's license and only five dollars in his pocket. He simply left the reservation and dropped in on their doorstep.

Unemployment on most reservations is 50 percent and can rise as high as 85 percent.[13] So many of the men are not working, and God placed the desire in a man's heart to work and provide for his family. When this is not happening, many of the men will think they are worth nothing and will begin to drown themselves in alcohol. That can subsequently lead to abuse, including sexual abuse and incest. One young boy who hung himself was being raped by a family member every day. He took all he could take before hanging himself.

Johnny Hughes realized that IMNA needed to start helping these young people beyond their spiritual lives and encourage them to see that they have value as human beings. He says many of the young people IMNA has reached sincerely love Jesus, but they are pretty clueless about the basics of life. They do not know how to handle money, balance a checkbook, complete an employment application, or look for a job, because they were not learning this at home.

The young people needed a strong foundation they can stand on when life gets rough, which includes a spiritual foundation. They also needed a foundation of life skills. Johnny says, "When the Israelites left Egypt, it took a while to get Egypt out of them. With these young people it is important to build relationships and trust, deal with their spiritual condition, and help them develop knowledge of practical living."[14]

These Native American youth also need to understand that they are part of God's huge tapestry, and He created every culture for a reason. For four hundred years the church has told Native Americans that they cannot be Native American and Christian. They were told that in order to be Christian, they must give up their culture and uniqueness—their clothes and traditional music and dance.

"I try to help the Native Americans understand that being a Christian does not mean giving up the way God created them or giving up their culture," Johnny says. "Yes, they might have picked up some traditions they should not continue to be involved with, and some might need complete deliverance and transformation in their spiritual lives. But if they choose to walk away from the way God created them, they leave a hole in God's tapestry.

"These and all other young people need to know that God created them with certain gifts and placed them in certain cultures for a reason. They have value and they can make a difference. It is important to teach them to reach out to other people and make a difference in the lives of others."[15]

A LIFE FALLING TO PIECES

Ailen grew up on the Navajo reservation and has been part of the mentoring and discipleship training under Indian Ministries of North America for five years. Raised in New Mexico, Ailen lost her father due to alcoholism when she was very young, leaving her mother to raise four children. Ailen's mother encouraged her children to stay in school and set goals for their lives, but when another man entered her mother's life, the children began to feel neglected.

Gradually Ailen felt that her life was falling to pieces. With her dad gone and her mother's attention focused elsewhere, she felt unwanted and worthless. Ailen recalls, "I longed for my mother's attention, like any young girl does. But it was as though I didn't exist anymore. My siblings remained drunk or high and fought all the time. Soon I was willing to do anything for my mother's love and attention."

At the age of twelve Ailen began to cut herself, hoping she would injure herself enough to force her mother to take her to the hospital. She explains, "I would hear a voice telling me to continue to cut, and to cut more and deeper. I was numb when I cut myself and would feel no pain. Now I know that it was the enemy trying to cause me to take my own life."

Indeed, cutting led to thoughts and plans of suicide. "I overdosed on pills twice in an attempt to die. One time my mother was so focused elsewhere that she just fed me some crackers and told me to move on."

At the age of fourteen Ailen became involved in a local gang, and her life continued to spiral out of control. Then a friend invited her to an Indian

Ministries of North America youth rally in Window Rock, Arizona. Ailen had attended church as a young girl, but she never had a relationship with Jesus or even understood who God was. "I went to that rally to escape my drunken siblings," she says. "But once I was there, I heard God's voice of love replacing the voice that tried to convince me to escape into death. I felt refreshed and alive!"

Now Ailen's message to every young Native American and anybody else who finds himself in a similar situation is this: "No earthly love can fulfill you. But there is a Father in heaven who loves you and does not want you to take the wrong path. Maybe love is missing in your life, but there is a greater love in Him than you will ever find, even through your earthly parents. Had people not reached out to me with the message of love and hope in Jesus Christ, I would probably be dead today."

Ailen's transformation also had an effect on her family, because God's love enabled her to be an example to them. She explains, "With constant prayer and faith, my family is not the same. I never expected to gain such a beautiful relationship with them. Mom and I are closer than before, and my older siblings have learned and grown into responsible adults with nothing but love for one another. I couldn't ask for more than what God is already doing. It's a blessing."

Today Ailen is a student at a Christian university, and her plan is to become a missionary to the Native American people so that she can share the story of the One who sacrificed His life for us.

THINGS TO CONSIDER

Suicide is never the solution. If you succeed, you have made an eternal and irreversible decision that also affects your surviving family members for a lifetime. They will be angry at you and possibly angry at God. They will be depressed, shocked, and numb. You will turn their world upside down, and you will always be remembered as the family member who committed suicide. That is not a good legacy.

Survivors suffer for a lifetime as a result of someone's suicide. Their lives are never the same as they deal with the painful loss. The suicide of someone close to them leaves unanswered questions and causes them to feel guilty, wondering if perhaps they could have done something to stop it.

If you attempt suicide and fail, you might be worse off than before. You could find yourself dealing with family problems, financial burdens, or permanent disabilities, all of which will compound your already-existing problems. Situations do not improve because you kill yourself or make a failed attempt.

It pains me to think that I could have left my wife alone with three children had I given in to those thoughts of suicide. My sons and daughter would have grown up without their dad. When I was being assailed by suicidal thoughts, I was so focused on my own pain, I didn't immediately think about that. If only people realized that suicide is a permanent solution to a temporary problem.

A depressed and suicidal person should realize that whatever crisis he is dealing with will pass. All problems have time limits, and later we will look back at past trouble and see it as just a bad memory. We will never deal with anything that somebody else hasn't already been through and recovered from. Always remember: this too shall pass.

That is the truth that finally broke through the fog of my pain and grief: *all problems have time limits.*

A SNOWBALL EFFECT

Three days before Christmas David and his family received a call in the middle of the night that shattered their world. David's stepmother called to say, "Your dad shot himself."

"Is he OK?" David asked.

"No, he is not," was the reply. "You need to get here right away."

"My first reaction was shock and disbelief," David said. "I had so many questions going through my head. How did this happen? How did he do this? He hasn't gone hunting this year. Was he cleaning his gun? Did somebody shoot him? All kinds of questions were going through my head. When I arrived at his house, the police would not let me in, perhaps because it was now considered a possible crime scene and needed to be investigated. One of my stepbrothers came outside and waited with me. Dad, still alive, had already been transported to the hospital.

"When I arrived at the hospital, Dad was in the intensive care unit. His head was swollen, and fluid was draining from his eyes and nose. It was evident there was no possible way he would survive without a miracle, although he did have an awareness of what was happening around him. I would say to him, 'If you can hear me, squeeze my fingers,' and he was able to do that.

"The decision was made to take Dad off life support, which was especially difficult for me because it did not matter to me if he lived in a vegetative state. I would have taken care of him for the rest of his life just to have him alive. After this decision was made, I left the hospital room and nobody knew where I had gone. My wife looked for me and found me on the floor, balled up in a corner, crying like a five-year-old. I had a meltdown right there in the hospital. Dad passed away early in the morning on Christmas Day."

About four months before the suicide, David's dad had been diagnosed with bipolar disorder. He had been institutionalized for two weeks, and before he shot himself, he had been placed on a new antidepressant medication.

"The week before Christmas Dad had been distancing himself from the family, even giving away some of his possessions," David said. "Every little incident seemed to be stressing him out and causing him to emotionally erupt. He had the idea in his head that nobody cared about him. We all thought he was being childish, but nobody realized he was going through some kind of depressive episode that might have been made worse by medication.

"Dad was depressed. His short-term disability had ended, and he did not get a job he had applied for. That might have been part of the source of his frustration. I felt like he thought he was doing people a favor by committing suicide.

"The night of the suicide the family had been

watching a movie when one of Dad's stepsons noticed that he was not around, so my stepmother left to check on him. She found him standing in a room with a gun pointed at his head. She yelled 'No!' and tried to pull the gun from his hand. He jerked his hand away, pointed the gun to his head again, and pulled the trigger."

For a while the family wondered if he really intended to shoot himself, or if he did so accidentally after being confronted.

"People usually leave a suicide note, but Dad did not. However, this was not the first time Dad had put a gun to his head. He did the same thing after he and my mother divorced. We discussed it then, and I told him, 'That is not the answer. You cannot do that to your children and grandchildren. That's being selfish.' Dad dealt with depression throughout his life, at least as far back as I can remember.

"Dad was a believer who was involved in our church, loved people, and was loved by those who knew him. Since he took his own life, I struggled as I wondered whether or not he made it to heaven. I asked myself the same questions I wanted to ask him: Why did you do this to me and my sister? Why did you do this to your grandchildren? How could you do this to your family, and do it right here at Christmas? I struggled with his suicide and death, but I did not discuss it much with anybody.

"I cried a lot, and my family noticed that I cried a lot. My youngest daughter was a small child at the time, and when she saw me crying, she would sit on my lap and try to comfort me. But I felt like I could not respond. I pushed my wife and children away because I didn't know how to deal with what I was going through.

"In the beginning I had a lot of guilt because my stepmother and I had talked about the possibility of putting Dad back in the hospital. But we decided to wait until after Christmas so he could spend Christmas with the family. When he died on Christmas Day, we all were beating ourselves up because we did not put him in the hospital before Christmas. We even considered that perhaps he had overheard us discussing another hospitalization and chose to shoot himself rather than be readmitted.

"The best way I can describe my feelings was disbelief in the beginning. It was as though I knew what happened, but my mind would not let me accept it or believe it. Dad had been my prayer partner, and I could talk to him about anything. He would give me sound advice, and when I was dealing with some issue and wanted him to take my side, he would say, 'Why don't we pray about it? Maybe you did the wrong thing.' When he died, it felt like I was losing more than one person. He was not just my dad, but my friend.

"Once everything hit me, I was angry at him for being selfish enough to do this to us. Emotionally I was numb and had a hard time showing my wife and children love. I could show affection to my dog, but I could not show affection to my own family. I became reclusive and even dealt with my own thoughts of suicide. It is hard to imagine how it is possible to have thoughts of suicide after seeing what my own dad's suicide did to the family. My family began to worry about me doing the same thing he did.

"I developed health problems, which most likely were stress related. I was placed on several medications, including antidepressants. Then, just a little over a year after Dad's suicide, I was severely injured in a single-car accident and suffered three contusions on my brain and a broken left femur, from which I now have a rod in my leg. I have no memory of two years of my life during that time. We vacationed at Disney World several months after the accident, and I do not remember being there. I have lost perception of time.

"On top of dealing with my dad's suicide, now I had my own problems to contend with. My children had lost their granddad, and now they felt like they had lost their dad. One time my son, speaking of me, used the terminology, 'When Daddy died.' That tore me up. He also loved his granddad and had a difficult time dealing with his death. I had kept my family at a distance after the suicide, and then after the accident my mind was affected. My wife and children seemed to think I was a different person. The person they knew was gone, and this other guy was here now, and he was someone they did not know.

"I went through a time when I had to deal with forgiveness. People would ask me, 'Have you forgiven your dad?' But it seemed ridiculous to forgive someone who was dead. It didn't seem possible or even relevant to forgive a dead person. I rationalized that it was not necessary. But I had a mini-breakdown that, combined with a sermon I heard about the importance of forgiving, made me realize I needed to forgive him. It was a surprise when the realization hit me, 'Wow, I need to forgive a dead person.'

"I did not start to overcome his suicide until I forgave him. It was strange to forgive someone who is dead. But it is important to forgive them, and to do it from your heart and not just from your mind. If I could say one thing to people, it would be that you need to forgive people who have hurt you, even if they are long gone. Sometimes without realizing it, we still hold anger and grudges against people who hurt us, even after they are gone.

"My wife was angry at my dad because of what his suicide had done to her husband and children. Because of the high doses of medication I was taking, I was so emotionally numb that I could not grieve. After the car accident, the doctors who treated me said the medication I was taking had caused a drug-induced slowing down of my brainwaves. The day of the accident I had left for work and was not even going in the right direction. I was headed in the opposite direction, toward a former place of employment.

"My wife tells me that I was literally in a drug stupor during that time. Perhaps I was, because I cannot remember much about my life during those three years. Only after that time did I finally grieve Dad's death. Looking back, I would say that people need to be allowed to go through the normal grieving process and not be medicated to numb their emotions. You are not clinically depressed just because you are grieving.

"My dad's suicide caused a chain reaction in our family. Our son changed from a happy-go-lucky child to a sad and angry boy who felt like he lost both his dad and granddad. He began to be bullied in school. I changed from a dad he had fun with to a man he did not recognize. My daughters stayed away from me so they wouldn't have to deal with it. My wife says I became angry and hard to deal with. Animosity developed because of my attitude.

"One person's decision to take his life had a snowball effect on the lives of the survivors."

HOW TO DEAL WITH THOUGHTS OF SUICIDE

In Mark 11:23–24 Jesus taught, "For assuredly, I say to you, whoever says to this mountain, 'Be removed and be cast into the sea,' and does not doubt in his heart, but believes that those things he says will be done, he will have whatever he says. Therefore I say to you, whatever things you ask when you pray, believe that you receive them, and you will have them." There is a twofold message in these verses that is applicable to this chapter.

First, don't ever say, "I'm going to commit suicide." Don't entertain the thought, and don't speak those negative words. When your heart and mouth come into agreement, things happen—either good or bad. Power is released in agreement.

God created our lives to work this way, and the adversary knows it. Spoken words are empowered in your mind, and your faith in your own destruction can more easily bring it to pass.

The enemy knows that if he can convince you to change your thoughts and your words, your own thoughts and words can and will be used against you. If you believe in your heart that your life will see destruction, then your own faith in your own destruction will enable it to more easily come to pass. Don't engage your heart in your own thoughts of destruction. Don't let the enemy build that stronghold in your mind.

I repeatedly quoted Philippians 4:13, "I can do all things through Christ who strengthens me," and verses such as 2 Corinthians 1:3–4, which says "God...[is] the God of all comfort, who comforts us in all our tribulation" (MEV); Psalm 50:15, "Call on Me in the day of trouble; I will deliver you" (MEV); and Romans 8:37, "In all these things we are more than conquerors through Him who loved us." Because I chose to agree with God's Word and refused to accept what Satan was telling me, the enemy lost his ability to torment me with suicidal thoughts.

Second, if you are dealing with depression and thoughts of suicide, pray and ask the Lord to help you. Pray, believe He will answer, and He will.

James 4:7–8 tells us, "Therefore submit to God. Resist the devil and he will flee from you. Draw near to God and He will draw near to you." This does not tell us to ignore the devil or come into agreement with him; it says resist him. Satan will always be your enemy, and he wants to see you defeated. His goal is to steal, kill, and destroy. Jesus gave us every spiritual weapon we need to overcome the attacks the enemy levels against us. We must learn to use our spiritual weapons before we need them. No soldier goes to war without proper training and practice. When an enemy attacks, the soldier must have already prepared in advance for the onslaught.

Some Christians think that once they are born again, the enemy will leave them alone. But that is not biblical. Look at how Satan attacked Jesus. He tried to tempt Him to sin, people tried to throw Him off a cliff, religious people attacked Him for His teachings, and so on. We cannot think that by ignoring the enemy, we will make him go away.

Perry Stone's dad told of an experience he encountered years ago when he pastored a church in North Carolina. He was in his office preparing a sermon for the following day when he felt a dark spirit enter the room. Suddenly thoughts of worthlessness began to bombard his mind, and the idea came to him that perhaps he should just end it all.

It did not take long for him to realize this was an attack of the enemy, and he began to take authority over it. The dark spirit left the room, but the next morning he learned that a neighbor had committed suicide that night. From that time on, he was convinced that, indeed, suicide can be the result of an attack by a murderous demonic spirit.

Clinical social worker Lisa Rathbun says, "In my work I have developed an informal theory regarding suicidal thoughts. It seems that thinking about death as an option to end pain begins rather innocently. However, it ends up being a portal into which demonic spirits can enter. Someone who says 'I wish I were dead' opens a door to allow demonic influence and torment. Over time that spirit, usually a murderous spirit, draws other tormenting spirits to it, thus strengthening the tormenting voices and convincing the host that suicide is a viable and perhaps the only option to end the pain."[16]

If you have friends or family who are depressed and suicidal, be a good listener. Suicide rates drop when people have someone they can talk with about their problems. Not everybody listens well to people who are depressed. Depression tends to make people self-focused, and many people, especially those who are positive and optimistic, have a hard time being around people who are depressed, suicidal, and self-focused. It steals their joy and makes them feel uncomfortable and unbalanced. But if you have an ear to listen, you are likely just the person they can talk with.

Most suicide attempts are expressions of extreme distress and not merely efforts to get attention. Anybody who seems to be suicidal should not be left alone and should receive medical and spiritual intervention as soon as possible.

A person who is dealing with thoughts of suicide must be reminded that problems have time limits. Whatever you are dealing with today will no longer be an issue one day. It too will pass. One day you will look back at the problem that seemed unbearable and insurmountable, and it will be nothing more than a bad memory. Maybe it will even be a humorous memory, and you might be thankful that things happened the way they did.

During the time that I felt depressed and suicidal, I isolated myself from family and friends, which I can say with certainty was the wrong thing to do. I urge you not to isolate yourself if you are going through some type of tragedy or loss or if a terrible event has happened to you. Stay near to your true friends and close family members. They love you and want to help you. Even though I did not want to be around people during this time, I learned that it was better to be around people and to talk about it.

I dealt with so many emotions that my reality became distorted. That is what happens when you become so caught up in your problems that you let your emotions control you. Reality becomes distorted when we begin to think the pain is permanent. That is a lie of the enemy. You will make it through this.

You might be going through something right now that seems guaranteed to destroy your life, but please believe me when I tell you there is hope. Jesus said in Mark 11 that if we will speak to the mountain, it has to move. Those mountains are compared to our problems. Problems seem big, but they are not too big for God. Always talk about how great God is, not about how big your problems are.

My future and my life seemed hopeless. When we begin to lose hope, we think outrageous and foolish thoughts. Since I was convinced that, ultimately, the accident was my fault, I became so hopeless that suicide crossed my mind at times as each new day seemed impossible to face. But as I took one day at a time, and as I prayed every day for God to help me, He answered my prayer. I tried to stay near to Him, although sometimes I felt distant from Him. But I took small steps at a time, and I recommend the same for others.

Anytime we want to know how to handle a situation,

we should refer to the Word of God, which is our foundation and source of truth. Let's look at two stories in the Bible involving people who, in the natural, could have lived out their lives with unforgiveness but instead chose to forgive. Because they did so, not only did God fight their battles, but also both people's lives were used to impact entire nations.

Chapter 9

MUST WE FORGIVE?

PEOPLE HAVE A range of opinions about forgiveness, many of which bear no resemblance to the teachings of Scripture. Some insist that you don't have to forgive at all. Others claim there is no need to forgive unless the perpetrator repents and makes restitution. Some say you should forgive only other believers, and then only if they first apologize. Still others say it is not only necessary to forgive but also that you must do so immediately.

Since the Word of God should be our source for truth, I want to spend this chapter looking at what the Bible tells us about forgiveness, beginning with two well-known examples of forgiveness from the Old Testament.

Beginning in Genesis chapter 37, we read about a young man named Joseph, one of twelve sons of the Hebrew patriarch Jacob (who was later renamed Israel). Joseph was his father's favorite child, and his brothers hated him because of his special relationship with their dad. When Joseph told his brothers about two dreams God had given him, his brothers envied him and later conspired to kill him. First they threw him into a pit. Then they decided to sell him to Ishmaelite traders for twenty pieces of silver, which was the price for a male slave under the age of twenty.

After committing the evil deed, the brothers returned home with Joseph's garment covered in animal blood and convinced their father that Joseph had been killed by a wild animal. Meanwhile the traders carried Joseph to Egypt and sold him to Potiphar, an officer of Pharaoh. Joseph was just a teenager, seventeen years of age at the time. And because of the evil actions of his brothers, he now found himself removed from his family and living as a slave in a strange land. Strike one.

Joseph had every reason to be angry. No doubt he was a frightened and homesick young man, but the Bible never indicates that he exhibited anger and unforgiveness. On the contrary, the Lord was with Joseph, and he became successful as he served Potiphar. Genesis 39:5 says that the Lord blessed Potiphar's house and field because of Joseph. As a result, he found favor with Potiphar and became overseer of his house.

Potiphar's wife had set her eyes on Joseph, but he refused her advances. In anger she lied about him, thereby causing him to be incarcerated in the king's prison. Strike two. But again, even though he was imprisoned for an act he did not commit, God showed Joseph mercy and gave him favor. Whatever he did, the Lord made it prosper.

While in prison Joseph was able to interpret the dreams of the chief butler and chief baker. The baker would die, but the butler would be restored to his position. In exchange for interpreting the dream, Joseph asked the butler to show kindness and mention him to Pharaoh so that he could get out of prison. But the butler said not a word. Strike three. Here was yet another opportunity for Joseph to be angry and unforgiving.

Two years passed. When Pharaoh had a dream that nobody could interpret, the butler suddenly remembered Joseph. He was brought before Pharaoh, where he interpreted the dream as a time of seven years of plenty followed by seven years of famine. Joseph suggested a plan for dealing with the famine, and because of his discernment, Pharaoh placed him second in charge in his kingdom.

The events happened as Joseph said, and during the famine Joseph's brothers journeyed to Egypt for food. You know the familiar story. Through a series of events Joseph tested his brothers and then revealed his identity to them.

Because of the favor that was upon Joseph, his entire family was permitted to move to Egypt. They were spared death and the family was reunited. Jacob's ancestors—the children of Israel—multiplied in the land until God used Moses to bring them out of Egypt.

Through the many ordeals that began when he was a teenager, Joseph had multiple opportunities to live with offense and unforgiveness. Sold into slavery by his own brothers, wrongly accused by his boss's wife, thrown into jail, forgotten by the butler, and left in prison for years, Joseph could have allowed a root of bitterness to grow. Imagine being in his shoes all those years!

When his brothers showed up in Egypt for food, Joseph could have shown them who was in charge now and allowed the entire family to starve to death. Instead he said, "God sent me ahead of you to preserve you as a remnant on the earth and to save your lives by a great deliverance. So now it was not you who sent me here, but God. He has made me a father to Pharaoh and lord of his entire household and a ruler throughout all the land of Egypt" (MEV).

I don't believe the Lord would have been able to use Joseph in this way had he been unforgiving and allowed himself to become bitter. Through Joseph's many trials God blessed him, gave him favor, and used him to save both the Egyptians and the children of Israel. Joseph's story teaches us that if we will allow Him to do so, God will take everything the enemy meant for evil in our situations and use it to accomplish something good—not just in our own lives, but also in the lives of those whom we might influence.

PURSUED BY A JEALOUS KING

The second life we will examine is that of David, a young shepherd who was anointed to be king over Israel when he was still a young man. Saul was king at the time, but he turned his back from following God and failed to fully obey God's commandments. When a distressing spirit troubled Saul, one of the servants brought David to play his harp so the spirit would depart. Saul liked David so much that he chose him to be his armor bearer.

When Saul and the men of Israel fought the Philistines, a giant named Goliath threatened them, and they were dreadfully afraid. Along came David, who confronted Goliath with a powerful word from the Lord, then knocked him out with a rock tossed from his slingshot and cut off Goliath's head using the giant's own sword. Saul was so impressed that he set David over the men of war.

But when they returned home, the women were in the streets dancing and singing, "Saul has slain his thousands, and David his ten thousands" (1 Sam. 18:7, MEV). Saul became jealous and afraid of David. Twice Saul tried to pin him to the wall with a spear. On another occasion Saul hoped David would be killed by the Philistines, but David prevailed. Then Saul gave David the wrong daughter as a wife—Michal instead of Merab. The king "became David's enemy continually" (1 Sam. 18:29). Even so, David behaved more wisely than all the servants of Saul, and his name became highly esteemed.

Saul asked his son Jonathan to kill David, but since Jonathan and David had become not just brothers-in-law but close friends, Jonathan warned David and told him to hide. The battle continued, with Saul threatening to kill David or asking other people to kill David and David being forced to flee for his life.

Saul even tried to kill his own son for protecting David. He had priests killed because one priest gave

David bread and Goliath's sword. David had to hide in the woods to protect himself from his own father-in-law. What would you do if your boss, who also happened to be your father-in-law, spent most of his time trying to kill you or have you killed because he was jealous of you?

At one point David and about four hundred distressed and discontented men who were following him decided to hide in the En Gedi wilderness. Saul heard about it and brought three thousand men to search for David. As they hid in the recesses of a cave, Saul entered the cave to attend to his needs. The men urged David to do to Saul as he saw fit, because surely the Lord had delivered him into David's hand.

Instead of harming or killing Saul, David chose to secretly cut off the corner of Saul's robe. But then he became troubled in his spirit for doing even that to the one who currently was anointed king of Israel. David confronted Saul with what he had done, just to prove that he meant him no harm. Had he intended to kill Saul, David could have done so in the cave.

While Saul was grateful that David spared his life, this still didn't stop him from coming after David again. David spared Saul's life one more time, even though he had ample opportunity to kill him had he so chosen.

Eventually Saul's sons—including Jonathan—were killed in battle against the Philistines, and Saul intentionally fell on his own sword after being severely wounded in battle (1 Sam. 31). When Saul died, God turned the kingdom over to David.

Look at the ordeal David endured before God's

promise came to pass. The king, David's boss and his own father-in-law, tried multiple times to kill him out of jealousy and fear, and David was forced to flee for his own life. David had many reasons to live in the flesh and become bitter, unforgiving, and vengeful. But David continued to follow God and honor Saul despite the way he was treated.

David made mistakes throughout his life, but he repented, was considered a great king, and was called a man after God's own heart. Why? Because he followed God with all his heart and obeyed God's will. (See 1 Kings 14:8; Acts 13:22.)

It is evident that neither Joseph nor David held animosity toward any of the people who wronged them. Joseph told his brothers not to worry about what they had done because God had it all under control. And when David learned that Saul was dead, he did not rejoice; he mourned.

Both stories teach us that we are not to become bitter and seek vengeance; instead, we should let God deal with the problem. Things will work out for the best if we give up the reins and let Him take control of the situation.

GETTING EVEN

Under the Mosaic Law of the Old Testament, the punishment for wrongdoing was harsh. Exodus 21:12–27 tells us that death was the sentence for murderers, for kidnappers who sold their victims, and even for children who cursed their parents. Leviticus 24:10–23 added a few more penalties. Blaspheming the name of the Lord would get you stoned to death. If you disfigured your neighbor, the same would be done to you.

If you bore false witness against your brother, judges would examine the case. If the person did indeed lie against a brother, the judges would "do to him as he thought to have done to his brother" (Deut. 19:19; see also verses 15–18). This punishment was so that other people would not be tempted to do the same thing, and this kind of evil would stop.

Much of the justice was an eye for an eye, tooth for tooth, hand for hand, foot for foot, burn for burn, wound for wound, stripe for stripe. Some commentators teach that this was implemented so that if you wanted to lawfully insist on punishment, the punishment could not be more severe than the crime. For instance, if somebody gouged out your eye, the same would be the maximum allowable punishment against the perpetrator.

Then Jesus came along and taught something that seemed to be contrary to the Law. He said: "You have heard that it was said, 'An eye for an eye, and a tooth for a tooth.' But I say to you, do not resist an evil person. But whoever strikes you on your right cheek, turn to him the other as well. And if anyone sues you in a court of law and takes away your tunic, let him have your cloak also. And whoever compels you to go a mile, go with him two" (MEV).

Jesus was telling us that instead of seeking revenge or retaliation, we should do something good in the face of evil. The *Matthew Henry Commentary* explains it like this: "We may avoid evil and resist it so far as is necessary to our own security; but we must not render evil for evil, must not bear a grudge, nor avenge ourselves, nor study to be even with those who have treated us unkindly, but we must go beyond them by forgiving them. The law of retaliation must be made consistent with the law of love. It will not justify us in hurting our brother to say that he began, for it is the second blow that makes the quarrel."[1]

In other words, we should not retaliate, using the reasoning, "You started it!" Retaliation begins a quarrel and increases the trouble between the two of you. Instead, react in love.

To further expound on the comments Jesus made, Matthew Henry explained that a blow to the cheek represents a hurt, affront, or indignity. What should we do in that case? Bear it, and don't dish out the same rudeness in return. Forgiving one injury might prevent another, because the two of you could end up fighting back and forth, which would accomplish nothing productive. Some people might ridicule you for not returning the affront, but those who are wise will honor you.[2]

The loss of a tunic represents a small matter for which somebody threatens to sue you in court. It is possible for bad people with no conscience, including judges, to take "the coat from a man's back." Just give him the coat for the sake of peace. It might cost you more to fight the case to keep your coat or have it returned to you than it would cost to buy a new coat.[3]

The last point Jesus made, to go an extra mile, refers to a wrong against your liberty. It is better to serve the person and avoid a quarrel than to serve your own lusts of pride and revenge.[4]

In summary, be charitable toward others and labor to do good things and no harm. Forgive the injury against you, and don't insist on any more punishment than is necessary for the public good.[5] The merciful will obtain mercy, and peacemakers will be called sons of God (Matt. 5:7–9).

I know from experience that forgiving those who have wronged us isn't easy, but obeying Jesus isn't an option for us as believers. I heard somewhere that unforgiveness is like drinking poison and hoping the other person will die. Our flesh doesn't want to give up the hurt; we want the other person to suffer as we have. But we'll never be free until we forgive.

I thought that by holding on to unforgiveness I was holding on to the fact that a wrong was done to me and my family, even if the courts didn't see it that way. I thought it was making me feel better about the situation, but it was killing me. That's what revenge does. It's like the story of the man who went out in the woods and was bitten by a poisonous snake. He could chase the snake and make it pay for biting him, or he could get treated for the snakebite. You can choose to chase the snake and let the poison of unforgiveness destroy you, or you can let it go and get to the Great Physician and be healed.

When I finally released the bitterness, resentment, hurt, and unforgiveness, I felt free. And with that freedom came peace, joy, and hope. Everything looked different. My future looked bright again. Everything looked better. This is why God wants us to put away unforgiveness (Eph. 4:31). It's not because God doesn't care about what happened. That's absolutely *not* the case. It's because unforgiveness destroys, and our loving Father wants us to have abundant life. He doesn't want the traumatic effects of the unexpected events in our lives to rob us of our destiny.

WHAT JESUS SAYS ABOUT FORGIVENESS

Jesus was not silent on the topic of forgiveness. In fact, He spoke of it often. Many times we don't want to accept Jesus's teachings, so we analyze His words and twist them to fit our personal circumstances or our theological beliefs. Or worse, we don't believe He really meant what He said.

But the Bible is clear about the importance of forgiveness. In Matthew 5:21–26 Jesus taught that murder begins in the heart. If we have anger toward our brother that is without cause and just provocation, if we are angry over groundless or trivial matters, or if we are angry with the intent to hurt the offender, then we are guilty of murder in our hearts! This is sinful anger, and it is a violation of the sixth commandment, "You shall not kill," which forbids murder, or the unlawful taking of life.

Even scornful words that are spoken with this kind of anger, malice, and hatred are a sin. The problem with this kind of anger and contempt is that it may indicate an attitude of the heart that places a person in danger of eternal punishment, according to Matthew 5:22.

Jesus continued the discourse by saying, "If you bring your gift to the altar and there remember that your brother has something against you, leave your gift there before the altar and go on your way. First be reconciled to your brother, and then come and offer your gift" (Matt. 5:23–24, MEV).

Unresolved conflicts do not go away by themselves. Jesus told us that if we find ourselves in that situation, we are to go and be reconciled with our brother "while we are on the way with him." (See Matthew 5:25.) That phrase means "while you are still alive." Be reconciled quickly in order to preserve Christian love and pursue peace and to keep you from dying before you reconcile and are forced to pay the penalty of justice. (See Matthew 5:25–26.)

What else should you do? Jesus said, "Love your enemies, bless those who curse you, do good to those who hate you, and pray for those who spitefully use you and persecute you, that you may be sons of your Father who is in heaven. For He makes His sun rise on the evil and on the good and sends rain on the just and on the unjust" (Matt. 5:44–45, MEV).

Then He asked, "If you love those who love you, what reward have you?" (v. 46). On the other hand, if we do as Jesus told us, we will "be perfect, just as your Father in heaven is perfect" (v. 48). The word *perfect* in this verse denotes wholeness and maturity.

In Matthew chapter 6 Jesus taught His disciples to pray. In verse 12 of what has become known as the Lord's Prayer, Jesus told them to pray, "Forgive us our debts, as we forgive our debtors" (MEV). A debtor is one who owes anything to another and has not yet made amends to those whom he or she has injured.

W. E. Vine's Concise Dictionary of the Bible says that such a debtor is someone whose disaster was liable to be regarded as due punishment. In other words, if something terrible happened to the debtor as a result of their actions, people might say they deserved it. Someone who sins and fails to live according to God's commandments becomes a debtor.[6]

When we pray this verse of the Lord's Prayer, we are asking the Lord to discharge, or forgive, the penalty of our sins. But notice that He tells us to ask Him to forgive us *in the same manner in which we forgive others!* When God forgives us of our sins, we are likewise expected to forgive those who sin against us.

Matthew 18:21–35 is known as the parable of the unforgiving servant. It begins with Peter asking Jesus how many times he is required to forgive someone who sins against him. "Up to seven times?" he asks.

Obviously Peter knew he must forgive. Jesus replied, "I do not say to you, up to seven times, but up to seventy times seven" (Matt. 18:22). Jesus was not stating a formula; He was saying, don't keep count. Keep forgiving. God forgives you no matter how many times you ask, and you are to do likewise.

Then Jesus told a parable about the kingdom of heaven being like a king who wanted to settle accounts with his servants. One servant owed ten thousand talents, which according to *Clarke's Commentary on the Bible* was "a myriad of talents, the highest number known in Greek arithmetical notation. An immense sum...equal to the annual revenue of the British empire!"[7]

The point was that this servant owed a debt that was so enormous he never could have repaid it. When the master commanded that he, his family, and all that he owned be sold to help repay the debt, the servant pleaded for patience. Moved with compassion, the master released him and forgave the entire debt he owed.

What did the servant do? He went out and found a fellow servant who owed him a hundred denarii and demanded that he repay. One denarius was a day's wages for a laborer. Putting this in perspective, one talent was equal to six thousand denarii. The forgiven servant had just been released of a debt equal to tens of millions of denarii—an unfathomable debt.

Yet when his fellow servant pleaded for patience, the forgiven servant took him by the throat, demanded repayment, and had the man thrown into prison until he could repay the debt. How fair was that?

The master heard about the actions of the forgiven servant and said, "You wicked servant! I forgave you all that debt because you pleaded with me. Should you not also have had compassion on your fellow servant, even as I had pity on you?" (Matt. 18:32–33, MEV). Angry, the master delivered the man to the torturers until he could pay all that was due. Since he owed a debt he could never have repaid, the wicked servant would never be free from the torturers.

Jesus ended with this warning: *"So also My heavenly Father will do to each of you, if from your heart you do not forgive your brother for his trespasses"* (Matt. 18:35, MEV, emphasis added).

What a sobering lesson in this parable! Each of us, because of our sin, owes a debt to God that we cannot repay. We are bankrupt debtors. But through the blood of Jesus and His death on the cross we can be forgiven of every sin and every insurmountable debt. We are loosed, and our obligation is canceled.

Any debt that we are owed by our fellow man pales in comparison to the debt of sin that we owe to a righteous God. He forgives us, and if we do not forgive our fellow man, then Jesus says we are wicked. When we were in distress, we pleaded for mercy and God showed us mercy. We are to show the same mercy to others. If we receive compassion, we are to show compassion.

What punishment did the wicked servant receive? A punishment equal to all that he owed—that is, the repayment of an immeasurable debt he could never repay. The punishment answers the sin; any person who does not forgive will not be forgiven. We are to forgive from the heart because the danger of not forgiving is, "So my heavenly Father will do to you." If you refuse to forgive and show mercy, you will suffer judgment without mercy.

No matter what someone has done to us, the truth is, we have no spiritual right to be unforgiving. We have been released from the chains of sin and forgiven a debt we can never repay. Jesus shed His blood so that our debt of sin could be paid. His love and compassion released us from our sin. In turn, God expects us to forgive others who have hurt us. This is not easy in our own power, but we can do all things through the strength of the Lord.

THE ULTIMATE ACT OF FORGIVENESS

The most significant act of forgiveness in Scripture is found in the crucifixion of Christ. We know that

Jesus bore our sins and died as the final offering for our redemption. He "bore our sins...on the tree, that we, having died to sins, might live for righteousness" (1 Pet. 2:24). The One through whom the world was created willingly laid down His life for the redemption of humanity and then was raised from the dead.

Jesus suffered horribly, as Isaiah prophesied He would be: "Surely he has borne our grief and carried our sorrows; yet we esteemed him stricken, smitten of God, and afflicted. But he was wounded for our transgressions, he was bruised for our iniquities; the chastisement of our peace was upon him, and by his stripes we are healed. All of us like sheep have gone astray; each of us has turned to his own way, but the LORD has laid on him the iniquity of us all. He was oppressed, and he was afflicted, yet he opened not his mouth; he was brought as a lamb to the slaughter, and as a sheep before its shearers is silent, so he opened not his mouth" (Isa. 53:4–7, MEV).

At the crucifixion of Jesus we find an example of two types of forgiveness. The first is forgiveness of our sins. This was displayed when one thief hanging on a cross pleaded, "Lord, remember me when You come into Your kingdom" (Luke 23:42, MEV). Jesus assured the thief that He would, indeed, be with Him in Paradise (v. 43).

Another type of forgiveness is found in Luke 23:34 when Jesus said, "Father, forgive them, for they know not what they do" (MEV). Despite the barbaric treatment He endured, Jesus forgave those who crucified Him. He prayed one last time for His enemies. He gave us a personal example and a final message about the necessity of both asking forgiveness for our sins and forgiving and praying for those who commit sins against us. Also, note that the people who crucified Jesus did not ask for forgiveness, but He forgave them anyway.

But this was *Jesus.* Surely God wouldn't command us to be like Jesus, would He?

People have all sorts of opinions about the importance of the command to forgive someone who has wronged them. Disagreement over an issue as serious as forgiveness should always be settled by referencing the source of all truth. So what does the Bible say about this issue? It tells us simply: just forgive.

Chapter 10

THE DANGERS OF UNFORGIVENESS

IT'S CLEAR IN Scripture that we should forgive, but knowing what is right is only half the battle. I knew I should forgive the young man involved in the accident that killed my family members, but for a time I wanted revenge. I wanted to see him pay. But I had no idea how that desire for vengeance was destroying me.

Every person who lives long enough will be wounded by somebody's words or actions, and when that happens, we can so easily allow ourselves to fall into bitterness and unforgiveness. But bitterness torments us, robs us of joy and peace, and cuts us off from the people around us. Bitter people live lonely and empty lives.

Hebrews 12:14–15 warns against allowing a root of bitterness to get into your spirit and your heart. We are to "pursue peace with all people, and holiness, without which no one will see the Lord: looking carefully lest anyone fall short of the grace of God; lest any root of bitterness springing up cause trouble, and by this many become defiled." It does not matter what happened to cause us to become bitter. It could have been a divorce, bullying at school, a failed business deal, someone in church who didn't treat us right, someone who slandered our name, someone who molested us, and the list goes on. If we remain bitter, we will suffer. Bitterness cuts off the power of God in our life and blocks God's blessings.

Forgiveness, on the other hand, draws people to us, heals and strengthens relationships, produces peace of mind, and releases God's anointing. Forgiveness is a stepping-stone to a greater dimension in Christ.

The moment somebody suggests forgiving the perpetrator, inevitably the victim's response will be, "How do you expect me to forgive someone who did that to me? I will *never* forgive!"

Is it difficult to forgive someone who has committed evil acts against you? Absolutely! Homicide, sexual abuse, adultery, verbal and physical abuse, and acts of depravity and rage that result in tragedy and trauma are not easy deeds to forgive—especially if we try to forgive in our own power. Scores of people have suffered horribly at the hands of others, with acts committed against them that can be hard to fathom.

Putting things in perspective, we realize that sometimes we allow ourselves to become angry and sin, even living with bitterness and unforgiveness, over petty infractions that should be brushed off and not entertained with a second thought.

Regardless of the reason for it, bitterness is like a

cancer that eats away at us. It will defile us and cause us to become resentful. It is toxic and deadly, but some people are not honest enough with themselves to admit they are living with bitterness and unforgiveness. They try to camouflage it with excuses such as "I just don't like that person," or "I just don't like their ways." Be careful, because there is a root of bitterness growing in your life, and when it springs forth, it will bring devastation.

Even in the church, marriages are falling apart because husbands and wives are bitter toward each other. They hold things inside and stew about them instead of dealing with the issues and resolving them, thus allowing the problems to grow worse and worse. Many second marriages end in divorce because one or both carry bitterness and unforgiveness from the first marriage.

I have heard people say, "My spouse cheated on me and I cannot get over it." But understand that this was the same condition you were in when you came to Jesus. We came to Him in a sinful state, meaning we were in the wrong. And yet His nail-scarred hands reached out to us as a bridge and not a barrier, and He said, "I will pick you up." Whatever has happened in your past, God wants you to humbly call out to Him and ask Him to dig up this root and remove it completely. Let go of the bitterness. He wants to set you free.

It's a Trap!

It is easy to fall into a trap of offense, bitterness, and unforgiveness. Once there has been an injustice or a hurt—whether intentional or unintentional—or even the perception of a hurt, negative emotions can rise, leading to the belief that we have been wronged. If instead of properly communicating with the person to deal with the hurt, we keep it inside, bitterness can take root.

We may also react to our hurt by avoiding or gossiping about the perpetrator. Most likely we feel anger churning within us. If this is allowed to grow into grudge holding, bitterness, and unforgiveness, we create a problem for ourselves that grows like a snowball rolling downhill.

Some people have been wounded in a very serious manner. We might have suffered through the murder of a loved one, or through rape, child abuse, molestation, or severe physical beatings. We know that we have been horribly wronged. We are in shock, pain, and disbelief. We feel physically sick. The enemy's fiery darts pierce our very being. We wonder, "How could this have happened to me?"

These emotions are understandable, but the enemy is waiting for you to fall into his trap. He enjoys planting seeds of offense, frustration, hurt, and injustice that produce a harvest of unforgiveness. If we are not on guard against it, the enemy will use these emotions to plant bitterness in our hearts, which will make our lives unfruitful and ineffective.

As I mentioned before, unforgiveness has been likened to drinking poison and waiting for the other person to die. Unless we are willing to deal with our wounds and hurts in a biblical fashion, we might find unhealthy ways to cope with the hurt, anger, and unforgiveness. Many choose to drown their pain with drugs, alcohol, promiscuity, or other addictions such as excessive shopping or overeating. Others deal with their hurt by lashing out at other people, perhaps in the same manner in which they have been hurt. One who was abused as a child, for example, might become a child abuser.

Signs of unresolved rejection, anger, bitterness, and unforgiveness include a short temper, hypersensitivity, and a critical spirit. Add to that any of the following: jealousy, shyness, speaking negatively about oneself, running from situations instead of facing them, changing jobs frequently, moving often, and being unable to retain friendships. Unfortunately many exhibiting these traits don't realize their behavior is linked to unresolved hurt that has led to bitterness.

Do you see the plot here? The enemy uses someone to harm you (or at least to plant in your mind the perception that you have been wronged). Then seeds of hurt are buried in your heart, and if not addressed through forgiveness, they will grow into bitterness and unforgiveness (Eph. 4:31). Your harvest will be sin and ruined relationships, which is exactly what Satan wants. Giving him an inch allows him to take a mile.

Those who are aware of the harm done to someone might see a connection between the hurt they suffered and the behavior they are now exhibiting. But refusing to believe there is a correlation means refusing to deal with the hurt, and that means refusing to receive emotional healing. Denial leads to discouragement, which can cause people to give up because they think things will never get better. When this happens, many people run away from life, perhaps by divorcing or even by choosing to end life altogether.

Those who are living with unforgiveness—whether they realize it or not—often have a victim mentality. They are preoccupied with the wrong committed against them, or with their perception that a wrong has been committed against them. As we will see, this behavior destroys health, friendships, marriages, families, careers, churches, and even the person's relationship with the Lord.

UNFORGIVENESS IS BAD FOR YOUR HEALTH

God created us; therefore, He knows that the mind profoundly affects the body. He knows that unforgiveness affects our health and can even place our very lives at risk. He knows that unforgiveness affects our relationships with other people *and* with Him.

Medical research confirms that bitterness, resentment, unresolved anger, and unforgiveness harm us physically.[1]

Each time we rehash the hurt against us—even by fantasizing about it—we harm our own bodies. Each time we fume and retell the story, we increase our hostility toward the person we believe wronged us. Every time we long for revenge, our bitterness and unforgiveness are killing us.

We should not think we are off the hook because we don't outwardly exhibit anger or because we don't have an explosive temper. Inner hostility and bitterness are just as detrimental as outward displays of anger. In both cases the anger, anxiety, and/or stress negatively affect the body.

Angry people suffer a host of physical ailments such as headaches, sleeplessness, panic attacks, high blood pressure, muscle tension, stomach and digestive problems, heart disease, increased risk of strokes, and suppression of the immune system that results in other serious illnesses, such as cancer. Anger and hostility will cause low heart rate variability and may be a predictor of sudden cardiac death, even among those who are free of heart disease. Hormones that negatively affect the body are excessively released in the bodies of angry people.[2]

Today we know that chronic anger and stress kill. Even holding grudges affects your health and decreases your life expectancy. Bitter, angry, resentful, and unforgiving people have a greater chance of dying early and are more likely to abuse drugs and alcohol.

Anger and unforgiveness also affect the brain. Even low levels of anger and resentment reduce cognitive function, cause an inability to think clearly and solve problems, and bring attacks of anxiety, panic disorders, and depression.

Relationships also suffer. Anger and negativity are carried into every relationship, even new ones. When someone is steeped in bitterness and unforgiveness, they cannot enjoy the present moment. Before I released my anger and bitterness, I struggled through several Christmases. I was physically there, but I was not able to fully enjoy my family. I tried hard not to show my pain, but it was tough, and I imagine my wife and children noticed.

Angry people do not connect well with others because it is difficult to befriend or live with habitually angry and resentful people. They often exhibit a "them against me" mentality, falsely thinking everybody is out to get them. They complain that life is not fair and make those around them miserable. Since misery loves company, these people won't have many close friends other than those who also spend their lives complaining and living in unforgiveness.

Along with his physical body, an unforgiving person suffers in his spiritual life as well. Unforgiveness closes off communication between us and God and opens the door for the enemy to operate. It will be difficult for an unforgiving person to sense the nearness of God, even when those around him are basking in His presence.

So many times as I stood in the pulpit, I felt totally empty. I had been trained to speak and preach, so I knew what to do, but there were many times when I did not feel God's presence on my life. By God's grace, the Lord ministered to the people despite me. When His Word goes forth, God does supernatural things. Miracles happened in those meetings because God's Word never returns void. But it certainly had nothing to do with me or the way I was feeling.

The Lord was clear when He spoke to me that day in the car that I could not go forward until I forgave. This was not a special word only for me. Although unforgiveness can cause a host of physical problems, those who live with a stronghold of unforgiveness will not find healing until they release their anger and bitterness. It does not matter how many prayer lines we stand in, how many times our name comes up for prayer in church, or how many times we pray for ourselves; we will not be healed until we deal with unforgiveness. Emotions related to bitterness and unforgiveness have such a detrimental effect on the entire body that some doctors claim that the majority of their patients would be healed of their conditions if they would only forgive those who have wronged them.

Not only will an unforgiving person not experience physical healing, but also one of the worst effects of unforgiveness is that it prevents us from achieving our highest calling in the kingdom of God. An unforgiving person will always have limitations placed on his life, perhaps not understanding but always wondering why he reached a certain point and could go no further. Getting stuck like this can lead to jealousy toward those who have reached higher goals in life, particularly if others have achieved the position or status we desired but failed to reach.

Unforgiveness robs us of our peace. It steals our joy. It keeps us from enjoying life and living with contentment. Unforgiving, angry, bitter, grudge-carrying people who are full of resentment will never live an abundant life in Christ.

Who suffers the most when we live with unresolved anger, bitterness, and unforgiveness? Is it the person we are holding in our mental prison? No, it is not. The person who suffers most is the person who refuses to forgive. Eventually the person living with unforgiveness will find himself locked up in a prison with the person he has not forgiven. He will be chained to the very person he believes has harmed him the most.

Why do we forgive? We do it to restore heath and relationships. We do it to bring back our joy and peace. Most importantly, we forgive because it brings us back into right standing with God.

WHAT EXACTLY IS FORGIVENESS?

In our hearts we know that it is important to forgive, but what exactly is forgiveness? People sometimes misunderstand the true definition of forgiveness, and perhaps that is why some think they can never forgive. What does it mean—and what does it *not* mean—to forgive?

First of all, forgiveness does not mean that we must deny that someone harmed us. It is a fact that something terrible happened and people are suffering. Forgiveness does not and should not involve denial.

Forgiveness does not mean that you condone a sinful act. We are *never* to condone sin. You are not expected to say to the perpetrator, "It's OK that you raped me, threatened me, and abused me." We don't forgive somebody for exhibiting evil traits; we forgive them for using their evil traits to harm us.

Forgiveness is something that happens inside our own hearts for our own benefit. Forgiveness changes you; it does not necessarily change the person who harmed you.

Because of what God's Word says, I knew I had to somehow forgive the other driver involved in the accident that killed my family. I knew God couldn't take me any further if I held on to bitterness. I knew

I had to get the desire for vengeance out of my hands and put it in God's hands, trusting that one day God would set the record straight.

But I wasn't compelled to forgive just because God tells us to do so. I felt like I couldn't carry the bitterness and anger any longer and I had to have some help somehow. I needed a miracle in my own heart. I told the Lord, "I have to let it go. Help me forgive. Free me. I give this to You. I'm not excusing what he did. I know what he did was wrong, but I've got to have some peace." When I prayed those words, I felt an immediate release and freedom. It was like somebody took a heavy burden and lifted it away.

After that point, when I thought about what happened, I never had the same perspective. I was no longer eaten up with a desire to bring the guy to justice. I'd left that in God's hands. I no longer to this day have ill feelings toward the man. That is the grace of God. That has nothing to do with me—that's Him.

Forgiveness should be like a canceled note. It should never be shown again. If I were to bring up the accident all the time, saying the driver needs to be punished, that's not forgiveness. Forgiveness says it's over. You can retain a memory of a hurtful event, but you no longer allow it to torment you. The act or situation doesn't define your life, and you don't constantly use it as a threat against the person who wronged you.

Forgiveness, however, does not mean that you should take the blame for someone else's bad behavior. Don't think that you caused it or deserved it, and don't assume that forgiveness means that you should allow the person to abuse and walk all over you again.

People are responsible for their actions. When you forgive, this does not mean that the person's crime or sin should go unpunished. It means that instead of dishing out our own form of justice, we allow punishment to be served by God, through proper legal channels, or both. We cannot take matters into our own hands and punish the one who harmed us. Vengeance belongs to the Lord. If we truly believe that God is in control, we can hand the problem to Him and allow Him to deal with it in the way He knows best.

Forgiving does not mean that you must forget. Often we hear that we should forgive and forget. But unless you become afflicted with dementia, some things will never be forgotten. I might forget a hateful remark that someone made to me, but how can I forget that a car accident killed three of my family members? Life-changing events will not be forgotten unless disease or injury wipes out your memory. To forgive simply means that you do not continue to rehearse the event in your mind.

When you have forgiven, you will not keep repeating what happened to nearly every person you meet. Forgiving means that when you see the perpetrator again, you will no longer feel anger and rage over what the person did to you.

Some wrongly assume that forgiveness commands that you establish or resume a relationship with someone who harmed you. That *could* happen, but that is not the purpose of forgiveness. Sometimes it is impossible, unwise, or unsafe to become involved in a relationship with the person who harmed you.

Conversely, we have all heard stories of someone

who committed a murder, went to prison, and was later contacted by the family of the murder victim. Through forgiveness and the love of Christ many of these families were able to lead the prisoner to a relationship with Jesus, which then empowers him to turn his life around. This is a perfect example of the biblical teaching of overcoming evil with good.

"What about trust?" you may ask. Forgiveness should never be considered a sign that you trust the person. Trust must be earned; it is not automatically given because you choose to forgive. Placing trust in or resuming a relationship with the person who harmed you could be an opportunity for you to be harmed again if that person's life has not been changed by the power of God.

So, how should we define forgiveness? Simply put, it means that you take the person out of your hands and place him in God's hands. Some have described forgiveness as taking the person off your hook and putting them on God's hook. You no longer hold them hostage in your mental prison. Instead, you release your resentment and anger to God and let Him, and, if possible, the legal system be responsible for serving justice and assigning punishment.

Forgiving someone means that we surrender any perceived right to get even or settle the score. The mere thought of vengeance may give us a sense of satisfaction in the midst of our anger. But again, it is not the perpetrator who is being harmed by these thoughts. It is the person who has chained the perpetrator in his mental prison.

Why do we have such a difficult time surrendering

our desire for revenge? Is it because we think God or the legal system will not be harsh enough? Is it because we want the person to suffer as much as we have? Or do we simply enjoy holding on to our victimhood status? Too often we hold on to old hurts that have nothing to do with the problem at hand. But because we have not dealt with them, we carry them as an added burden everywhere we go.

When my family died in the car accident and the trial ended as it did, I felt the young man did not pay for his actions. To me, the trial was unfair and seemed to be rigged in his favor. But by holding on to that anger, what was I hoping for? Did I hope the driver would spend the rest of his life behind bars? Did I want the young man to lose someone he loves so he could know how I felt? We should ask ourselves: What do we expect when we seek revenge? If that person suffers, do we really think that will solve our problem?

Who was harmed by my anger? Did it harm the driver? Certainly not. I harmed myself and my own relationships. I had to forgive him to set *myself* free. This is an important point. You forgive the person and remove him from your mental prison, not to set *him* free, but to set *yourself* free.

Sometimes an unforgiving individual makes the person who sinned against him pay and pay and pay. For years—sometime for a lifetime—they make the person pay. Punishment takes the form of accusations, critical comments, hostility, or physical abuse. The person who was harmed might continually remind the offender of the wrong that was committed, never letting the person live it down. While this behavior might indeed make the perpetrator's life miserable, it also makes the victim's life miserable. Nobody wins in these situations.

Should you demand an apology? Or forgive only if the person comes to you and apologizes or begs your forgiveness? A previous chapter noted that Jesus exhibited the proper example for us when He hung on the cross and prayed that the Father would forgive those who crucified Him, even before any of them apologized or asked forgiveness.

To demand an apology before you forgive is a form of pride and self-righteousness, which also is a sin. Forgiveness, on the other hand, is an act of obedience to God. We cannot always expect an apology. And we cannot wait until we get one to practice forgiveness.

LET'S SHRUG OFF MINOR OFFENSES

Let's consider minor offenses. A minor offense might be words that someone spoke to you or about you that made you angry. This wouldn't necessarily be a slanderous remark or a lie that defames your character; it might be gossip, or even a comment meant to be harmless. Regardless, it made you angry. But let's keep offense in perspective by remembering that we all have many chances in life to be both the offended and the offender.

Minor offenses should never be allowed to grow into bitterness and unforgiveness. What should we do about these offenses? I suggest that we ignore them. Develop patience or a thicker skin. Unforgiving people are easily offended, and they tend to nurse and rehearse their hurts, no matter how insignificant and no matter how long ago the incident occurred. Generally these people are swift to complain and find fault with others, and quick to be offended.

We all have personality quirks, and some people are more eccentric than others. People annoy us and say things we don't appreciate; this is a fact of life. But instead of being offended, Christians are called to display consideration, patience, and love. If we would simply learn to communicate, we would find that proper communication can fix most of these problems.

Let's shrug off minor offenses and stop being hypersensitive. We are all flawed human beings who have offended people at some point, whether intentionally or unintentionally, knowingly or unknowingly. Sometimes we say or do things that we immediately regret, but since we were not created with rewind buttons, it is impossible to erase what has already been said or done. God is merciful to us, and we should be merciful to others.

If you find that you are easily offended, or that people must carefully examine everything they say and do around you so that you will not become offended and angry, it is time to examine your life in light of Scripture. Learn to be more accepting of people and their faults and differences. If it is a trivial offense, don't let it get into your spirit and affect your life. Pray that the Lord will help you display more of the fruit of the Spirit in your life—love, joy, peace, longsuffering, kindness, goodness, faithfulness, gentleness, and self-control (See Gal. 5:22–23).

For those who know people who have truly been the victim of another's cruel and vile behavior, remember that it is easier to tell the victims they need to forgive than it is to practice the act of forgiveness. Physical and emotional scars can last a lifetime.

What does it take to forgive? I forgave only by the grace of God. I was filled with so much anger that I wanted to *shoot* the guy. To say that I am a fourth-generation minister who wanted to shoot someone in revenge is a terrible confession. By thinking such a thought, I had already committed murder in my heart.

To some degree, I think many of us have been in similar circumstances. Who *hasn't* sinned in anger and needed to forgive? Who *hasn't* been the person who needs to be forgiven? Let this become firmly rooted in your spirit: we must learn and practice forgiveness, because unforgiveness is a stronghold that the enemy uses to gain entrance to our souls.

Forgiveness is an attitude of the heart toward the person who needs to be forgiven. If we harbor unforgiveness in our hearts, God will deal with us about it until we either take action and forgive, or until we become so obstinate that we refuse to listen any longer. God expects us to repent of our sin of unforgiveness toward the person we are holding hostage.

The question then becomes: How do we forgive? Keep reading. We will examine this important question in the next chapter.

Chapter 11

HOW DO I FORGIVE?

WE MIGHT ASK ourselves why we must be the ones to forgive, since we were wronged. But understand that God wants us to separate the sin committed against us from the person who committed the sin. Our battle is not against flesh and blood, but against the spirits that control people who sin against others. The apostle Paul wrote of this in Ephesians 6:12: "For our fight is not against flesh and blood, but against principalities, against powers, against the rulers of the darkness of this world, and against spiritual forces of evil in the heavenly places" (MEV).

Bitterness, rage, and unforgiveness should not be directed toward the perpetrator, because he or she is being controlled by evil spirits and powers of darkness. If you live with sinful attitudes, your own actions open the door for you to be influenced and tormented by the adversary.

As with grief, you will likely move through a couple

of stages before realizing you need to forgive. At first you might be in shock and disbelief at the person's actions or the tragic outcome of events. Forgiveness might not cross your mind at that moment.

Then you become angry and your problems escalate. You might lash out at or distance yourself from the offender. The individual or the situation will consume your thoughts, and you will repeat the problem over and over to those around you until your own relationships begin to suffer. Regardless of the offense, you want people to empathize with you and help carry your burden, even though God did not assign most of them to help you carry it.

Forgiveness Is a Choice

As previously stated, forgiveness is an act of the will, not the emotions. So how can you take steps to forgive? Allow me to offer the following tips:

Don't repeat, repeat, repeat

One of the first steps to forgiving someone is to realize that forgiveness is an act of your will and not your emotions. One of the best ways to move toward forgiveness is to control your emotions and stop rehashing the incident over and over. Persistent repetition of the story, sometimes until others are tired of hearing it, is self-destructive. Some nurse and rehearse the incident for a lifetime, choosing to remain stuck there instead of doing the right and healthy thing and moving beyond it.

We must choose to make a conscious decision to stop reliving the event. Recalling the grievance over and over rekindles our anger, which destroys not only our life and health but also the lives of those around us.

If we find ourselves living with destructive bitterness and unforgiveness, or a desire to get revenge, we have reached that crossroads where we and others know it is time to choose the right path and deal with the problem. If you are that person, now is the time to unchain the hostage and release your anger and rage. Know that you can forgive, and determine in your heart to do just that. I am not saying this comes naturally. I am not suggesting it is easy. We don't forgive because it is natural or easy; we forgive because it is a biblical command.

I once heard a minister say, "Emotions that are not subject to biblical thinking tend to run amok and cause great damage." Conquer your emotions and refuse to let them run amok and control your life. Forgiveness is healing—to your body, soul, and spirit. Since there is always an element of free will in our decisions, as believers in Christ we should always examine our emotions and our responses in light of Scripture.

Take it to the Lord

We should ask the Lord to help us release and forgive. It is difficult to forgive in our own strength, but we are able to forgive and release through God's supernatural grace. We can do all things through Christ who gives us strength (Phil. 4:13). When the Lord confronted me, I prayed, "Lord, I cannot do this on my own, so You are going to have to help me release this and forgive." He answered my prayer, and He will do the same for you if you reach out to Him.

God will also heal your memories and emotions and give you peace, joy, or whatever is missing in your life. Just ask. Tell Him that you do not want your emotions to ruin your life and health and poison your relationships with Him and others.

Ask God to help you give up any perceived right to get even and settle the score. He will help you do your part to live at peace with everyone. Do not repay evil for evil or avenge yourself, because vengeance belongs to the Lord.

Romans 12:17–19 tells us, "Repay no one evil for evil. Have regard for good things in the sight of all men. If it is possible, as much as depends on you, live peaceably with all men. Beloved, do not avenge yourselves, but rather give place to wrath; for it is written, 'Vengeance is Mine, I will repay,' says the Lord." To give place to wrath means that you move over and let God handle it. He cannot defend you as long as you are standing in front of Him trying to defend yourself.

If you are unable or unwilling to ask God to help you overcome this problem, then this is a good indication that you have become obstinate in your sin. This is a spiritually dangerous place to be. The first step in this situation is to humble yourself and repent, thereby getting your heart right with God before you are able to ask Him to help you forgive someone.

My mother had to deal with unforgiveness as well. I will let her share her experience in her own words:

My husband was a prince of a man, and when we arrived that day to visit our son and his family, little did I know that within twenty-four hours I would be a widow, losing the love of my life, my mother, and my grandmother, who was like a second mother to me. I lost my husband, our life's work, and our home. I moved out of the church's parsonage and into the home with my son David and his wife, Lisa. I was lost without my husband. We had been married thirty-three years.

One night I went to dinner at a friend's house, and other ladies were there visiting and sharing. My friend shared with the ladies what had happened and asked them to pray with me. One lady asked me if I had forgiven the driver of the other car. I replied, "I have just been trying not to hate him." A lady suggested that when we pray, I should tell God that I forgive this driver and ask for His help in forgiving.

I did just that, and God began to help me forgive. I felt heaviness lift off me, and I began to get better. Unforgiveness will cause a person to have many problems, including health problems. Forgiveness helps us to heal. Mark 11:25 tells us that if we hold anything against someone, we are to forgive them so our Father in heaven will forgive us of our sins.

It has been over twenty years since the accident, and God has opened doors of work, friends, and a wonderful church. In 2013 the Lord brought a wonderful, godly man named Durand Faircloth to be my husband. Things happen that we do not understand, but God never fails us. And oh, how He loves us.

Overcome evil with good

Romans 12:20–21 tells us to feed our enemy when he is hungry and give him drink when he is thirsty, for this will heap coals of fire on his head! Do not be overcome with evil, but overcome evil with good. Only when you are willing to surrender to the Lord your desire for revenge, and only when you are willing to forgive the person who wronged you will you begin to receive healing.

Repent of rebellion

Jesus told us that we must forgive if we want to be forgiven. We reap what we sow, and we cannot sow evil and reap good things, or sow unforgiveness and reap forgiveness. To disobey and continue in unforgiveness is rebellion. Believing you have a right to get even is rebellion.

We are told in 1 Samuel 15:23 that rebellion is as the sin of witchcraft. When we are rebellious, we don't care that we are sinning; we simply want to be in control. But we must give up that desire to control. To refuse to give up control and let God handle the situation is stubbornness, and that same verse tells us that stubbornness is as iniquity and idolatry.

Demanding control of the situation means that we do not believe God can handle it or that we don't want to accept His form of justice. When we do this, we are placing ourselves in a position above God. And that is not the place to be.

Ephesians 4:26–27 tells us, "Be angry but do not sin. Do not let the sun go down on your anger. Do not give place to the devil" (MEV). When you fail to obey this command, and when you engage in unrighteous anger with the desire to harm someone or get revenge, you give up your own territory to the enemy. You also appear foolish and immature.

Continuing in verses 31–32, Paul wrote, "Let all bitterness, wrath, anger, outbursts, and blasphemies, with all malice, be taken away from you. And be kind one to another, tenderhearted, forgiving one another, just as God in Christ also forgave you" (MEV).

Remove anger, bitterness, wrath, and malice from your life. Forgive. Tell God that you are placing it at His feet because you refuse to be saddled with it any longer.

Regardless of what the Scripture says, some people refuse to forgive, or to even believe that forgiveness is necessary. Some say it is unwise or even impossible to forgive. But why would Jesus tell us to forgive if it is unnecessary, unwise, or impossible? Some of the greatest stories ever told have been stories of forgiveness. Here is one that was so powerful, it was reported in national news and later was produced as a film.

THE AMISH EXAMPLE

A tragic event occurred several years ago that resulted in an astonishing—and some said shocking—example of biblical forgiveness. On October 2, 2006, a thirty-two-year-old gunman entered an Amish schoolhouse in Lancaster County, Pennsylvania, and released several boys before taking ten children hostage.[1]

The shooter indicated that he intended to shoot the hostages. Hoping to buy time for a rescue, two sisters, ages eleven and thirteen, requested that they be shot first and the others be allowed to go free. Both sisters were shot; one died and the other lived. The gunman shot the rest of the hostages, killing four more girls. One of the survivors suffered terrible brain injuries and is wheelchair-bound, unable to talk or walk.[2] The gunman then turned the weapon on himself and committed suicide.[3]

While America's eyes were on the community, a grandfather of one of the murdered girls warned some of the young Amish people not to hate the killer. Another father said, "He had a mother and a wife and a soul, and now he is standing before a just God."[4]

The murderer left a suicide note for his wife and each of his children, claiming that he had molested two young female relatives when he was twelve and was having dreams of molesting again. He also claimed he was angry at God.[5]

Instead of being angry at the murderer, the surprising response of the Amish community was to reach out to the man's wife and children. Within hours of the tragedy an Amish neighbor was comforting the murderer's family and extending forgiveness. Others in the community visited the family, with one Amish man holding the killer's father in his arms as the man sobbed for an hour. Some even attended the murderer's funeral. In another surprising act of kindness the Amish set up a charitable fund for the family of the man who murdered their children.[6]

The response of Marie, wife of the murderer, shows the reason God commands that we forgive. Marie wrote an open letter to the Amish in the community, thanking them for their forgiveness, grace, and mercy. She wrote, "Your love for our family has helped to provide the healing we so desperately need. Gifts you've given have touched our hearts in a way no words can describe. Your compassion has reached beyond our family, beyond our community, and is changing our world, and for this we sincerely thank you."[7]

The Amish were publicly criticized for being too quick to forgive, even though the killer was dead and the Amish were simply reaching out to another family that was also suffering. People were certain the forgiveness must be insincere and certainly undeserved. But scholars of Amish life explained that forgiveness is deeply rooted in the Amish culture. Many of their Anabaptist ancestors in sixteenth-century Europe were torturously martyred for their religious beliefs, so forgiving the enemy has always been engrained in their whole community. They believe as the Bible teaches—that forgiveness does not undo the tragedy; it is merely a first step toward a more hopeful future.[8]

In an interview with National Public Radio, Professor Donald Kraybill said, "The Amish certainly would've also forgiven [the killer] if he would still be living. If he would've been imprisoned, I'm sure they would've made some efforts to visit him...[the Amish] don't assume responsibility for meting out justice...they would say...it's our responsibility to forgive, but it's up to the police and the system of justice to deal with punishment."[9]

Kraybill explained that the Amish forget the wrong in this manner: once someone has been forgiven, they believe it is bordering on being sinful to keep talking about it and repeating it. This is not to say it is erased from their memories; they simply choose not to keep rehashing the event.[10]

This does not mean that the Amish who lived through this tragic event did not have to deal with a range of emotions after the shooting. Some of the boys who were released from the schoolhouse wondered if they could have done something to stop it, and some received counseling. Forgiveness does not mean you will not suffer through the stages of grief.[11]

Is There a Secret to Forgiveness?

The Amish understand faith and love. Those who understand and have experienced God's love and forgiveness have an easier time loving and forgiving others. Unfortunately, perhaps through life's circumstances, some people do not know or believe that God loves them. Yet it was because of His love that He provided a way for our sins to be forgiven!

In the Old Testament God established a system of sacrificial offering through the blood of perfect and spotless animals. The animals became a substitute for sin and a picture of the coming Messiah and His offering for our redemption.

From the foundations of the earth God had a better plan for the future. Jesus came to earth, knowing that He would ultimately die as the final substitute offering for the redemption of our sins. After that, according to Hebrews 10:3–4, it became impossible for the blood of sacrificial animals to take away sins. Only through the blood of Jesus can your sins be completely blotted away, as though they were never committed.

God provided a way for us to be forgiven and reconciled to Him. Regardless of what you have done, He seeks relationship and restoration. You have not been too bad for God to forgive you. Following the same path, He wants us to forgive and, as much as possible, be reconciled with others.

Through our own sin of not forgiving others, our relationships are broken. Our unforgiveness leads to death—the death of the relationship with that person and the death of our spiritual relationship with Christ. Our method of restoration is forgiveness.

When somebody acts in harmful ways toward us, we must understand that what is done is done. Once the act is performed, it cannot be undone. Once the words are spoken, they cannot be taken back. I could not rewind the day and change the situation to bring my family back. Once something is done, we have two choices. We can either become bitter and unforgiving, or we can become better and forgive. Choose to forgive, and then pick up your life and move forward.

We do not receive God's forgiveness by our works. Likewise, when we forgive others, we should not require penance, restitution, or suffering before we forgive them. God will always provide deliverance and freedom for those who forgive from their hearts. Ephesians 4:32 tells us, "Be kind to one another, tenderhearted, forgiving one another, even as God in Christ forgave you." It requires a tender heart to be able to forgive those who have wronged you.

How Will I Know I Have Forgiven?

People struggle with the question, Have I really forgiven? They wonder how they can know when they truly have forgiven someone. Any of the following are indications that you still hold unforgiveness toward somebody:

1. You still mentally and verbally rehearse the offense that was committed against you, perhaps even decades after it occurred.

2. Even though you have no reason to do so, you find yourself disliking people who have the same physical or personality traits as the person who offended you.

3. You refuse to take responsibility for your own actions because you blame your bad behavior on the perpetrator. You might use the excuse that you would be a better person today had it not been for the one who harmed you.

4. If you have contact with the perpetrator, you still attempt to make his or her life miserable by criticizing him, reminding him of what he did to you and exhibiting an unloving attitude.

5. You believe the person does not deserve forgiveness.

6. You do everything possible to keep from coming into contact with the person.

7. You are so selfishly concerned with your own rights and feelings that you do not see the need to forgive.

8. You still want to get revenge.

9. Sometimes you need to forgive yourself. If you have not forgiven yourself for actions in your past, you will harbor guilt, self-hatred, a belief that you do not deserve to be forgiven, and an opinion that you have been so bad that even God will not forgive you.

10. Another way to gauge forgiveness is to note any harsh feelings you have toward the person when you see him, when he comes to mind, or when his name is mentioned. If you still have anger toward that person, it is likely that you have not fully forgiven.

A woman told the story of seeing a Facebook post from another woman who had been involved in a sordid affair years ago with her first husband. She thought she had forgiven the woman, but the moment she saw her name, she realized she still harbored ill feelings toward her. In that moment all of the old emotions of anger and bitterness returned.

She got off Facebook and tried to get the woman off her mind. She prayed, "Lord, I thought I had forgiven her, but now this old hurtful pain and the ugly thoughts have returned. It is hard for me to even see her name again."

To her surprise the Lord told her to befriend the woman. She couldn't believe what she was hearing and said, "Oh, no, Lord, that cannot be from You!" But the thought was very clear and very strong, and she knew she had to befriend the woman.

After pondering all night whether to respond to the direction she sensed from the Lord, she sent the woman a Facebook friend request. The woman accepted and sent her a message telling her that she had been thinking and praying about her for years because she had always been haunted by her past actions and regretted the hurt she had caused.

The woman was in tears, and in that moment she sensed the Holy Spirit pouring His love into her for the other woman. She no longer felt any hurt or bitterness, but only love. All those other feelings were suddenly gone. The woman replied back and told the other woman that she forgave her, and she encouraged the woman to also forgive herself. Both women were once victims, but they became victors through forgiveness.

God wants to see us healed and whole, not stuck in unforgiveness. Unforgiveness is rooted in anger. Have you ever known people who always seem to be angry at somebody, people who always seem ready to explode? The Bible warns us, "Make no friendship with an angry man, and with a furious man do not go, lest you learn his ways and set a snare for your soul" (Prov. 22:24–25). If you cannot let go of unforgiveness, perhaps you first need to release your anger. God does not want you to be angry and sin, so He will help you overcome anything that you truly release to Him in prayer—including anger.

What If I Was the Offender?

When we are the person who has harmed or wronged someone, here is what we should do: repent to God, apologize to the individual harmed, and attempt to make things right.

Our first step should be to go before God and repent for our sin. Then go to the person and own up to your behavior without rationalizing it, making excuses, or placing blame. Tell the victim you have asked God to forgive you for your terrible act, and you are asking him to forgive you as well.

Some counselors suggest this process for talking with the victim:

1. Say, "I'm sorry for how I have treated you (or the things I've said or done, or views I have held about you and attitudes I have exhibited)."

2. Ask the person to please forgive you.

3. Tell the individual wronged that you love him or her, if you sincerely do.

4. Thank the person for his forgiveness.

5. Ask God to change your heart toward that person and for Him to change the person's heart toward you.

6. Change your behavior! Everything said in this process will be nothing but empty words if you continue to engage in the acts that caused the trouble in the first place. Do not expect the victim to trust you again until you prove that you can be trusted.

Unforgiveness Among Christians

We as Christians need to deal with unforgiveness within the church. Many Christians hold offense against other Christians, and some hold it for years or even decades. Churches split and friendships are destroyed over offense and unforgiveness. People leave the church and might never return because someone offended them.

The Bible gives us a simple way to deal with those in the church who sin against us. Matthew 18:15–19 teaches that we should go to the person and attempt to get the matter straightened out through simple and clear communication—not through accusation or anger or gossip. The offended person begins the process, and the goal is to clear up the problem and reconcile. Your goal is not to throw the offender under the bus.

If that does not work, take someone with you the next time, and make sure it is someone who is a neutral party. Do not take a friend who has sided with you, carried your offense, and is prepared to help you gang up on the other person. This causes even more trouble, gossip, and dissension. Take someone who can mediate the situation and help the two of you resolve it.

When that does not work, the Bible makes provision for us to take the problem to "the church" for resolution. I do not believe this means that we should stand up in front of the congregation and unload the problem or call everybody we know and gossip about the situation. It might mean the pastor should get involved at this point.

However, let it be known that the church should not have to get involved in petty quarrels and squabbles. Every disagreement or ill-spoken word cannot be turned into an offense. Some Christians simply need to grow up and develop thicker skin. Others need to learn to control their tongues and show more patience and love.

Anytime we confront someone about a sin they have committed against us, we should do it with the goal to get things straightened out and not to harm the other person or seek revenge. We are to speak the truth in love and not be arrogant, self-righteous, or haughty. Remember that we need to get the plank out of our own eye before we attempt to remove the speck from our brother's eye. By the same measure that we judge, it will be measured back to us (Matt. 7:1–5).

Don't harbor grudges and misunderstandings. Don't go to others and gossip, expecting them to take your side. Just do the biblical thing, and go to the person and try to straighten things out.

Keep a tender heart toward others. Live with a constant spirit of forgiveness. Each time we forgive, we release a bondage we have carried. Each time we are forgiven, a burden is released from upon us.

We cannot allow the enemy to take a smoldering ember and turn it into a blazing fire that destroys everything and everyone around us. Act quickly to control the ember before you allow it to destroy your health, relationships, and spiritual walk with God.

TAKE THE LOAD OFF

When we finally choose to forgive, we are able to walk in peace and freedom. God removes the baggage we've been holding, and our load is lighter. This is what my friend experienced. I asked her to share her story in her own words:

> My earliest childhood memory was that of seeing my dad go to prison. My family always told me that he went to prison for carrying a concealed weapon, but later I learned that he was a drug dealer. I saw pictures of him standing behind marijuana plants, and the only thing visible besides his face was the beer can he was holding. The day he went to prison, he hugged us, kissed us, told us good-bye, and then he left. I cried, my mother was upset, and my brother became a very angry young man.
>
> After that it seemed that a spirit of depression hovered over our house. Mom worked three jobs to support us, and she also attended college to get a business degree. We seldom saw her unless we went to work with her, or when she took us to her school, where we would run up and down the halls while she was in class.
>
> For a while an aunt stepped in to babysit us, but as we grew older we became latchkey children. At age seven my brother molested me and began to beat me up every day—knocking me down the stairs, hitting me with a belt or anything else he could find, punching me, or throwing darts at my head. I was afraid to tell anybody, so people thought I was a klutz because I was always covered with bruises. I grew quiet

and distant, and students at school were also picking on me and knocking me around.

By the age of nine I was retaliating by beating on my own mother. At times she called the police so somebody could get me off her. I was angry because she was supposed to be protecting me, yet she was not. I couldn't understand why nobody was protecting me.

I gained a lot of weight, and I hated it when people would tell me, "You have such a pretty face. You would be attractive if you would just lose weight." My mother told me I was dumb and stupid and that I was going to be a bitter old nun and nobody was ever going to want me. Day in and day out I was told how worthless I was until I finally believed it.

Eventually I started abusing myself and even tried to slice my wrists in front of my mother. I thought I was so stupid I couldn't even succeed in killing myself.

At thirteen I started drinking after my brother gave me rum and Coke. While I didn't particularly care for drinking, I drank because it made me feel accepted by people. I also started smoking pot. Around this same time I was raped by the older brother of a girl I was babysitting, and then by a cousin's boyfriend. I was even molested by my own brother.

Things did not go well after Dad was released from prison. The day he threw his socks and shoes in my face and told me to put them on him was the day I walked out of the house.

When I was twenty-one, I moved to Tennessee because I was miserable and knew that I needed to get away. I had become a hermit and weighed over four hundred pounds. I packed a few things and left at three o'clock in the morning, headed to a university where I had not even enrolled. Thankfully they accepted me on a probationary basis and told me I would have to prove myself if I wanted to stay. After my first semester they accepted me and took me off probation.

I started attending a church near the university, but I was an angry, hateful, and bitter person. One weekend the church gave me the opportunity to attend an Encounter weekend. The leaders were very caring, and I noticed that these women had a peace about them that I did not have. When I heard the testimony of one of the women, I said, "Lord, if You can bring her through what You have brought her through, then You can help me. If I have made it this far, You can help me keep pressing on."

A week later I began to work at a camp with children who had been physically abused and abandoned. The Lord began to show me purpose and that He could use what I had been through for good. I was able to give these children love and attention in a godly manner, as somebody who did not have to love them but still loved them willingly and unconditionally. That gave me fulfillment. I said, "OK, Lord, now I know You can use what I have been through to help others."

I changed from a bitter, angry young woman who was manipulative and a pathological liar, from alcohol, drug use, and promiscuity, to a woman who loves and fears God and wants to serve Him at all times in everything I do. I began to accept myself and learn that God does not make junk, no matter what people told me. The Lord loves me, and I was learning to love myself.

The Lord also dealt with me about unforgiveness. For a while I could not look at my parents without remembering how verbally abusive they were to me. When I returned home one Christmas, my dad got angry and came at me with a twelve-inch knife. I froze. Mom stood between us, and Dad threatened to send me to hell where I belonged. Mom was able to distract him long enough to allow me to get to my car. She ran to the car, yelling that this was my fault.

At first I didn't recognize the need to forgive my parents. But the Lord made me see that I needed to forgive not just them, but myself for the different things I had put myself through—the self-mutilation and so on. He helped me understand that it was not my fault that my parents treated me the way they did. When I came to respect myself and could place myself in the role of a godly woman, I was able to establish boundaries with my parents. Through that I was able to forgive them. But first I had to forgive myself and learn who I am in Christ.

As I forgave myself and began to change, my appearance changed. Not only did I lose weight, but with no more hatred and bitterness, my countenance also changed. When my heart changed, people could see it in my eyes.

To those who are dealing with similar things, I want to remind you that we do not have to bear the shame of our youth. Jesus carried it; therefore, we don't have to bear it. I had to be open to what He had for me. When someone told me I was inadequate, I had to learn to say, "No, I am not. Jesus makes me adequate." When people say I am stupid, I say the Lord gives me wisdom. When people say I am unworthy and weak, I remind myself that the Lord says I am worthy and strong.

This has not been easy, but anything worth having is not easy. The more you speak the truth of God's Word over yourself, the more you will believe it. And the more you believe it, the more your life will change for Christ, and the easier it will become to forgive those in your life who have hurt you.

MAKE FORGIVENESS A PRIORITY

The longer you let unforgiveness remain in your life, the deeper it is buried and the harder it will become for you to deal with it. The greater hold it gets on you, the tighter its grip becomes. It will become like a snake that coils around its prey and squeezes the very life out of its victim.

Sadly many people accept unforgiveness and make it part of their life. Their spirits become stubborn, and they spend the rest of their lives behind the bars of a prison they have created for themselves. While they once might have been close to Christ, their unforgiveness has caused them to break fellowship with Him, and they are left with no anointing and a cold, hard shell of religion. I believe unforgiveness among Christians is one reason the power of God is limited in our churches.

Forgiveness is not optional. It is not something you do if you feel like it. Those who stubbornly refuse to forgive are in willful disobedience and spiritual jeopardy. Some people are so obstinate that they will allow offense to carry them to hell. Is it worth it? It has been said that he who will not forgive others burns the bridge on which he must pass to get to the gates of heaven.

Forgiveness gives a new start—a fresh beginning. Surrender your will to His will, and let the Spirit of the Lord transform your heart.

Chapter 12

LESSONS TO LEARN

LOOKING BACK TO the time of the accident, I am thankful beyond words that our son Matt was healed and was able to fully recover, and that my mother survived with no life-threatening injuries. But I had rough and challenging days as I tried to move past the grief of losing family members, especially Dad.

He was only fifty-eight years old when he died. I was thirty-two, and I thought he should have lived a long life—at least another twenty years. But his life was cut short on the highway that night.

I knew that I should have died in that accident because the Honda was aimed directly at us. Our car was totaled, yet every person walked away unscathed. Because of the location of the impact on our car, I could have died in that crash. Yet I lived while my dad died.

For too long I was held captive by guilt and regret,

unable to forgive myself for taking the shortcut instead of the interstate. I was continually tormented by the question, What if I had not been so eager to get home early and had taken the interstate instead of the shortcut?

I continued to preach, but only because that was my occupation and I had to care for my family. I spent many nights at the pulpit simply going through the motions. I can see now that the enemy was plotting to take me out, and he uses the same tactics on many others.

For quite a while after the accident I was gripped by a fear of driving. But one night about two years after the accident I was in a service where Perry Stone was preaching. He called me out of the congregation and told me, "The Lord said to tell you that He is going to put an angel on the bumper of your car." Immediately fear left me. From that moment on, I was never again afraid to drive. To this day I have no fear.

WARNING SIGNS

A couple of years after the accident Perry told me that in April of 1992, his own dad, a Church of God minister who also happened to be named Fred Stone, dreamed of seeing a terrible accident on the very same road my family traveled that night. He sensed in the dream that someone was killed after being hit by a drunk driver. Knowing that Perry was traveling back and forth along this road during the revival, he had warned Perry to be careful. In a bizarre chain of events an accident that could have killed me, or even

Perry had he continued the revival, instead killed another Church of God minister named Fred Stone.

This brings me to the topic of warning signs from the Holy Spirit. Some people don't like warning signs, but they are everywhere. Signs warn us of speed limits, railroad crossings, dangerous animals, deadly chemicals, and all sorts of things. If we ignore the warning signs, we do so at our own peril.

God gives us warning signs too. Yet when He gives a dream, a vision, or a prompting of trouble on the horizon, many people close their ears and do not want to hear it. When God gives someone a warning or a burden, many people convince themselves there is nothing to it. Other times people are too busy and distracted to hear the Lord telling them to stop, listen, and pray. I believe my dad fell into that last category.

Earlier in the book I mentioned that my family arrived at our home late because of car trouble. In retrospect, this was most likely warning sign number one. Sometimes we gripe about delays and find a way to avoid them when we should instead thank God for the delay. He may be trying to protect us from trouble down the road, and if we will listen to Him and obey, we could save ourselves much grief. Had Dad not been too distracted to listen, perhaps he would have prayed and the Holy Spirit might have warned, "Turn around and go back home. This is not the right time to make this trip."

Also, recall that the closer he came to our home, the more troubled he became in his spirit. It was as though he had a sense of foreboding that something terrible was going to happen. This was warning sign number two—the most powerful warning that should have been heeded immediately.

A third attempt might have been when I asked Mom and Dad to stay home and enjoy their time with the children. Had they not gone to the revival that night, they would have been out of harm's way. After church I would have returned home to be with my family instead of eating at Shoney's, so I would have been off the highway by the time the driver approached the dangerous curve.

Here is a crucial lesson for every person reading this. Please latch on to this, even if you learn nothing else from this book. Any time you have a burden or a foreboding sense that something terrible is going to happen, pray immediately. In my dad's situation the proper action would have been to say, "I am heavily burdened about something, and I believe the Lord wants us to stop right now and pray." Then pull off the road, or stop what you are doing, and pray. Keep praying until the burden lifts and you get a release from the Lord that your prayer has been answered.

I cannot let myself off the hook here, either. When Dad told me about the car trouble and the heaviness in his spirit, I should have been sensitive enough to the Holy Spirit to say, "Let's pray about that, Dad, and see if the Lord will reveal the reason for your burden."

Always be aware that the enemy makes his plans, but God allows the Holy Spirit to warn us and deliver us from the plans of the enemy. However, we must *listen* to the warnings and *pray* until the burden lifts.

Perry's own family was involved in a serious automobile accident in the early 1960s that taught his dad this lesson. Both of his parents were severely injured in a two-car collision at a time when there was no such thing as seat belts. When his dad prayed from the hospital room and asked the Lord why He allowed the accident to happen, the Lord said, "I tried to stop you three times, but you didn't pay attention."

Thinking back, he recalled that a deer had walked onto the highway, stopped, and stood in front of his car. Instead of waiting for the deer to move, he drove around it. The second attempt occurred when the Holy Spirit prompted him to take a shortcut, and he did not listen because his wife warned him that the road was in terrible condition. The third time, just as he neared the turnoff to the shortcut, the Holy Spirit prompted him again to take that road. He did not obey, and moments later they rounded a curve and were involved in a serious accident that, oddly enough, involved a drunk driver.

Always pay attention to the promptings of the Holy Spirit. A heavy, oppressive feeling in your spirit is a sign that you should immediately stop whatever you are doing and pray. Do not ignore it. Do not wait. It could mean that the enemy is making destructive plans, and your intercession is vital to stop it. Pray until the burden lifts, no matter how long it takes. Your prayers could save somebody's life—even your own.

If you are a believer, you must never be too busy or distracted to listen and pray. God will send warnings to protect you, but you cannot ignore them.

JUSTICE IS NOT IN YOUR HANDS

Sudden death or other such unexpected events caused by others are tragic and life-changing for those affected, but knowing that justice was not served makes dealing with this even more difficult. Human nature demands justice.

The writer of Ecclesiastes wrote about this. Ecclesiastes 3:16–17 says, "Moreover I saw what was under the sun: In the place of justice, there was wickedness; and in the place of righteousness, there was wickedness. I thought in my heart: God will bring judgment to the righteous and the wicked, for there is an appropriate time for every matter and deed" (MEV).

Then we are told in Ecclesiastes 5:8, "If you see the oppression of the poor, and the violent perversion of justice and righteousness in a province, do not marvel at the matter; for high official watches over high official, and higher officials are over them."

In other words, injustice is not a good thing, but it is a common thing, so you might as well expect it and do not be shocked when it happens. Even government leaders who should uphold the law are guilty of perverting justice and righteousness, and this could go all the way up the chain of command.

But ultimately the time will come when God will judge both the righteous and the wicked. Even if it does not seem to happen in this lifetime, it will happen in the next.

The apostle Paul wrote in 2 Timothy 4:14, "Alexander the coppersmith did me much evil. May the Lord reward him according to his works" (MEV). The Lord will always deal with people on our behalf, because as He said, "Vengeance is Mine, I will repay" (Rom. 12:19). He alone has the right to vengeance.

If we feel that we have been wronged and justice has not been served, one of the worst things we can do is step in front of God and attempt to handle it ourselves. This will never work in our favor.

Writing about Romans 12:17–21, the commentator Matthew Henry said: "When a man's passion is up, and the stream is strong, let it pass off; lest it be made to rage the more against us. The line of our duty is clearly marked out, and if our enemies are not melted by persevering kindness, we are not to seek vengeance; they will be consumed by the fiery wrath of that God to whom vengeance belongeth. The last verse suggests what is not easily understood by the world; that in all strife and contention, those that revenge are conquered, and those that forgive are conquerors. Be not overcome of evil. Learn to defeat ill designs against you, either to change them, or to preserve your own peace. He that has this rule over his spirit, is better than the mighty."[1]

THE OFFENDER IS HUMAN TOO

We are all created in the image and likeness of God, and He put us on earth for a reason. When people do or say things that hurt us, we tend to no longer see their humanity through their faults. We don't view them as people made in the image of God; instead, we see only evil and the influence of the enemy. But God wants us to see past their faults and look at their potential in Christ.

When the young man involved in the accident that killed my family left his home that day, I am certain he did not say, "I think I'll get into a car accident tonight." He left school after taking an exam, went to a bar, drank with friends, and drove home at a time when he probably should not have been driving. Our lives were forever changed that night, and his life probably was too in some way.

The day he entered the courtroom, he was facing a prison sentence for negligent homicide and assault. If convicted, his years of college would have been wasted.

In my high school years I was an athlete, and the boys on my team drank nearly every weekend. We attended parties, and one other guy and I were the only two who would not drink. Many nights I had to drive intoxicated classmates home because in their drunken state they would have become a dangerous weapon on the highway. One wrong move behind the wheel and lives would have been permanently altered in an instant.

I do not recommend that a person drink alcohol, but if you insist, then never drink and drive. Young people are particularly vulnerable because they are naïve enough to think they are invincible. They don't have enough driving experience to know how to handle emergency situations, yet they drink and sit behind the wheel of a three-thousand-pound vehicle and think they can control it under any circumstances.

Remember that every fifty minutes someone dies in a drunk-driving accident. The average drunk driver has driven while intoxicated eighty times before his first arrest.[2] But as terrible as someone's actions might be, sometimes we need to look through a different lens at the people who have wronged us. Instead of self-righteously pointing our finger at them, we must see them through God's eyes. We should realize that, were it not for the grace and mercy of God, we could be walking in that person's shoes.

FACING ETERNITY

It has been said that if you ask a group of people how many want to go to heaven, everybody will raise their hands. If you ask how many want to go today, nobody will raise their hands. Everybody wants to go to heaven, but nobody wants to go today, and nobody wants to die to get there.

It sounds cliché, but life truly is fragile. Nobody has a guarantee that somebody they know and love will not slip into eternity today. As much as we may not want to face death, we have a guarantee that, unless we are alive to see the return of the Lord for His people, the day will come when each of us will die. Statistics tell us that more than one hundred fifty thousand people die each day.[3] That means every second two people die and face eternity. Some will be ready; many will not. My dad, grandmother, and great-grandmother were ready to face eternity. They are all in the presence of the Lord today. Of that I have assurance.

While death is a fact of life and nobody wants to die, we know that death is merely the process of leaving this earthly and corruptible body while the soul and spirit enter another destination. Death is not the end;

it is the beginning. When those who are born again in Christ die, they will find themselves in the presence of the Almighty, along with the heavenly angels and all the children of God who have already passed on.

The day of Dad's funeral I looked at his grave and questioned life. Today I look back and think of Jesus on the cross when He cried out, "My God, My God, why have You forsaken Me?" (Matt. 27:46). Yet at the end He cried out, "Father, 'into Your hands I commit My spirit'" (Luke 23:46) and then, "It is finished" (John 19:30). But we know that His death was not the end; it was the beginning. As difficult as it is to accept the death of someone dear to us, when that person has a relationship with Jesus, death is not the end.

When believers in Christ die, they immediately go to a better place. The good news is that we have the opportunity to see them again. The only requirement is that our sins be forgiven and we remain in right relationship with Christ. As believers we have assurance that the next time we see our friends or loved ones, we will be reunited for eternity. Nothing will ever separate us again.

To put this in proper perspective, isn't eternity with our Savior the ultimate goal? Every believer who understands what is ahead looks forward to that day when tears will be wiped away and there will be no more sorrow. Some people just arrive there sooner than others.

While it is true that a tragic event might take us to heaven, it is also true that going to heaven is not a tragic event. On that fateful night Dad passed from this life and immediately entered the place he had preached about and longed for. There he saw his Savior face-to-face. He entered a place of indescribable peace, joy, and perfection—a place that we cannot begin to imagine. I don't think that my family members would choose to return to this earth under any circumstances; instead, they will wait patiently for the rest of us to arrive.

There is a time to be born and a time to die, and I believe it could be possible to leave this earth before your appointed time. Still, our purpose is not to question God or become angry. Our purpose is to learn from the tragedy and find a way to glorify God through it all. If the events that transpired and the lessons learned through Dad's death can bring blessing, hope, healing, or salvation to others, then his death will not have been in vain.

I read about a family who lost three of their four children in one tragic event. Even as one son was dying, the mother stroked his hair as she cried and kept repeating, "God, You are faithful, true, and good in all Your ways...no matter what!"[4]

That is a lesson we must learn. We all will experience situations and trials that we never wanted or expected to face. But through it all God still loves us, and He is still faithful. He is right there beside us and He will see us through any trouble we face in this life. He will walk us through the trials if we allow Him to take the reins of our life instead of turning them over to the enemy. I speak from experience when I say that God will see us through and He will heal our broken hearts. Don't give up on God; He has not given up on you.

Some of our greatest victories come through our

praise and thanksgiving to God as we stand firmly in these fiery trials. It takes abundant faith and trust in Him to say, in the midst of it all, "Father, I might not understand why this is happening, but You are a good and faithful God, and I know You will walk with me through this battle and never let me down."

When we can speak praise and thanksgiving during these worst of times, we are truly offering to God a sacrifice of praise. Even during our tests, troubles, and trials we can say, like the psalmist, "I will offer to You the sacrifice of thanksgiving, and will call upon the name of the LORD" (Ps. 116:17).

ARE YOU READY TO FACE ETERNITY?

Not one of us is promised tomorrow. Not one of us is promised another moment in this day. Yet we make plans for tomorrow while neglecting the single most important decision we will make in this life—the decision about where we will spend eternity.

Sin is a reality for human beings. We all have violated the commands and standards of God. We all need God's forgiveness in order to have our sins erased and receive His gift of eternal life. How do we receive forgiveness for our sins? The Bible tells us:

> If you confess with your mouth Jesus is Lord, and believe in your heart that God has raised Him from the dead, you will be saved, for with the heart one believes unto righteousness, and with the mouth confession is made unto salvation.
>
> —ROMANS 10:9–10, MEV

Therefore repent and be converted, that your sins may be wiped away, that times of refreshing may come from the presence of the Lord.

—ACTS 3:19, MEV

If we confess our sins, He is faithful and just to forgive us our sins and cleanse us from all unrighteousness.

—1 JOHN 1:9, MEV

When you believe, confess, and repent with a sincere heart, God will blot out your sins as though they never existed. Don't delay any longer. Make Jesus the Lord and Savior of your life today.

Here is a prayer of salvation and cleansing that you can pray right now:

Heavenly Father, thank You for loving me and sending Your Son, Jesus, to die on a cross and carry my sins. I confess that I am a sinner. I accept Your gift of salvation, and I ask You to forgive me of all my sins and give me eternal life. Cleanse me of all wickedness and unrighteousness. Remove bitterness, unforgiveness, anger, strife, pride, greed, rejection, and rebellion from my life. I forgive and release those who have harmed and wronged me. Cleanse me of everything I have been involved in that is ungodly in Your sight. Break every stronghold of the enemy over my life. Break the power that I have given the enemy over my soul. Help me to live righteously according to Your Word. I accept the victory and freedom that I now have in

Christ Jesus. Thank You for giving me eternal
life. In Jesus's name, amen.

The Bible also tells us to be baptized in water after we pray a prayer of salvation: "He who believes and is baptized will be saved" (Mark 16:16). Don't neglect this important step.

Begin to read the Bible, and spend time each day praising and thanking God for everything He has done and is doing in your life. Develop a prayer life. He wants to help you in your daily walk with Him. Just ask. Keep a humble and repentant heart so that the enemy will not gain another foothold in your life.

Always remain faithful to the Lord, and may He bless you and bring peace and joy into your life as you continue your walk with Him.

NOTES

Chapter 3
The Aftermath

1. *Cleveland Daily Banner,* "Highway Patrol Says Driver Crossed Over Center Line," May 1, 1992.
2. Ibid.

Chapter 4
Seeking Justice

1. Allen Mincey, "Prosecutors Say McClure Intoxicated," *Cleveland Daily Banner,* April 28, 1993.
2. Ibid.
3. Ibid.
4. Ibid.
5. Allen Mincey, "Deliberations in McClure Case to Begin Today," *Cleveland Daily Banner,* April 29, 1993.
6. Mincey, "Prosecutors Say McClure Intoxicated."
7. Mincey, "Deliberations in McClure Case to Begin Today."
8. Ibid.
9. Ibid.
10. Ibid.
11. Allen Mincey, "Jury Says McClure Not Guilty in Fatal Traffic Deaths," *Cleveland Daily Banner,* April 30, 1993.
12. Ibid.

Chapter 5
Life Goes On?

1. The Center for BrainHealth, "Study Finds Aerobic Exercise Improves Memory, Brain Function and Physical Fitness," November 12, 2013, http://www.brainhealth.utdallas.edu/blog_page/study-finds-aerobic-exercise-improves-memory-brain-function-and-physical-fi.
2. Ibid.

CHAPTER 6
OVERCOMING GRIEF

1. C. S. Lewis, *The Complete C. S. Lewis Signature Classics* (New York: HarperCollins, 2002), 445.
2. Leon F. Seltzer, "What Your Anger May Be Hiding," July 11, 2008, http://www.psychologytoday.com/blog/evolution-the-self/200807/what-your-anger-may-be-hiding (accessed November 20, 2014).
3. Don Colbert, *Stress Less* (Lake Mary, FL: Siloam, 2005).
4. Ibid.
5. MADD.org, "Drunk Driving Statistics," http:www.madd.org/drunk-driving/about/drunk-driving-statistics.html (accessed December 30, 2014)
6. FoxNews.com, "Police: 1981 Murder of Son of America's Most Wanted Anchor John Walsh Is Solved," December 17, 2008, http://www.foxnews.com/story/0,2933,467905,00.html (accessed November 20, 2014).
7. Daniel G. Amen, *Change Your Brain, Change Your Life* (New York: Three Rivers Press, 1998), 44.
8. Amie M. Gordon, "Up All Night: The Effects of Sleep Loss on Mood," *Psychology Today*, August 1, 2013, http://www.psychologytoday.com/blog/between-you-and-me/201308/all-night-the-effects-sleep-loss-mood (accessed November 18, 2014).
9. *Science Daily*, "Scientists Find Brain Areas Affected by Lack of Sleep," November 14, 2003, http://www.sciencedaily.com/releases/2003/11/031113065511.htm (accessed November 18, 2014).
10. Harvard Health Publications, "Exercise and Depression," http://www.health.harvard.edu/newsweek/Exercise-and-Depression-report-excerpt.htm (accessed November 20, 2014).
11. Gina Shaw, "Water and Stress Reduction: Sipping Stress Away," WebMD, http://www.webmd.com/diet/features/water-stress-reduction (accessed November 18, 2014).
12. Daniel G. Amen, *Change Your Brain, Change Your Life* (New York: Harmony Books, 2010), 234.
13. Ibid., 227–229.
14. *Courageous*, directed by Alex Kendrick (Culver City, CA: Sony Pictures Home Entertainment, 2012), DVD.

15. C. S. Lewis, *Mere Christianity* (New York: HarperCollins, 2001), 115.

CHAPTER 7
THE DARKNESS OF DEPRESSION

1. Anxiety and Depression Association of America, "Facts and Statistics," http://www.adaa.org/about-adaa/press-room/facts-statistics (accessed November 20, 2014).
2. Healthline, "Unhappiness by the Numbers: 2012 Depression Statistics," http://www.healthline.com/health/depression/statistics-infographic (accessed November 20, 2014).
3. Centers for Disease Control and Prevention, "An Estimated 1 in 10 US Adults Reports Depression," http://www.cdc.gov/features/dsdepression/index.html (accessed November 20, 2014).
4. Alice G. Walton, "The Gender Inequality of Suicide: Why Are Men at Such High Risk?" *Forbes*, September 24, 2012, http://www.forbes.com/sites/alicegwalton/2012/09/24/the-gender-inequality-of-suicide-why-are-men-at-such-high-risk/ (accessed November 20, 2014).
5. *Science Daily*, "Global Depression Statistics," July 26, 2011, http://www.sciencedaily.com/releases/2011/07/110725202240.htm (accessed November 20, 2014).
6. Lisa Rathbun, in communication with the author.
7. Ibid.
8. Amen, *Change Your Brain, Change Your Life* (1998).
9. Ibid.
10. Amen, *Change Your Brain, Change Your Body* (2010), 147–148.
11. Ibid., 27–28.
12. Daniel G. Amen, *Magnificent Mind at Any Age* (New York: Three Rivers Press, 2008), 96.
13. Mayo Clinic, "Stress Relief From Laughter? It's No Joke," July 23, 2013, http://www.mayoclinic.org/healthy-living/stress-management/in-depth/stress-relief/art-20044456 (accessed November 20, 2014).

14. Caroline Leaf, *Who Switched off My Brain?* (Southlake, TX: Improv, Ltd., 2009), 15.
15. Ibid., 36–37.
16. Ibid., 15.
17. Ibid., 20
18. W. E. Vine, *W. E. Vine's Concise Dictionary of the Bible* (Nashville, TN: Thomas Nelson, 2005), 310.
19. Rick Renner, *Sparkling Gems From the Greek* (Tulsa, OK: Teach All Nations, 2003), 448.
20. Adam Clarke, *The Holy Bible: Containing the Old and New Testaments, the Text...*vol. 3 (New York: T. Mason & G. Lane, 1837), 739. Viewed at Google Books.
21. Leaf, *Who Switched off My Brain?*, 29.
22. Lisa Rathbun, in communication with the author.
23. Kenneth Cooper, *It's Better to Believe* (Nashville: Thomas Nelson, 1995), 5.

CHAPTER 8
AN IRREVERSIBLE DECISION

1. Centers for Disease Control and Prevention, "Suicide: Facts at a Glance 2012," http://www.cdc.gov/violenceprevention/pdf/suicide_datasheet-a.pdf (accessed November 20, 2014).
2. Paula Span, "Suicide Rates Are High Among the Elderly," *New York Times*, August 7, 2013, http://newoldage.blogs.nytimes.com/2013/08/07/high-suicide-rates-among-the-elderly/?_r=0 (accessed November 20, 2014).
3. Centers for Disease Control and Prevention, "Suicide: Facts at a Glance 2012."
4. National Institute of Mental Health, "Suicide: A Major, Preventable Mental Health Problem," http://www.nimh.nih.gov/health/publications/suicide-a-major-preventable-mental-health-problem-fact-sheet/index.shtml (accessed November 20, 2014).
5. M. Asberg, "Neurotransmitters and Suicidal Behavior. The Evidence From Cerebrospinal Fluid Studies," *Annals of the New York Academy of Sciences*, December 29, 1997, http://www.ncbi.nlm.nih.gov/pubmed/9616798 (accessed November 20, 2014); J. John Mann, "Neurobiological Aspects of Suicide," New York

State Office of Mental Health, 2012, https://www.omh
.ny.gov/omhweb/savinglives/Volume2/neurobiological
.html (accessed November 20, 2014).

6. Span, "Suicide Rates Are High Among the Elderly."
7. National Institute of Mental Health, "Suicide in America: Frequently Asked Questions," http://www.nimh.nih.gov/health/publications/suicide-in-america/indcx.shtml (accessed November 20, 2014).
8. Centers for Disease Control and Prevention, "Suicide Prevention: Youth Suicide," http://www.cdc.gov/violenceprevention/pub/youth_suicide.html (accessed November 20, 2014).
9. Centers for Disease Control and Prevention, "National Suicide Statistics at a Glance," http://www.cdc.gov/violenceprevention/suicide/statistics/rates03.html (accessed November 20, 2014).
10. Johnny Hughes, in communication with the author.
11. Ibid.
12. Ibid.
13. RT.com, "Native American Poverty Continues Under Obama," http://rt.com/usa/usa-native-american-poverty-obama/ (accessed November 20, 2014).
14. Johnny Hughes, in communication with the author.
15. Ibid.
16. Lisa Rathbun, in communication with the author.

CHAPTER 9
MUST WE FORGIVE?

1. Leslie F. Church, ed., *Matthew Henry Commentary of the Bible* (Grand Rapids, MI: Zondervan, 1961), 1225.
2. Ibid.
3. Ibid., 1226.
4. Ibid.
5. Ibid.
6. W. E. Vine, *Vine's Concise Dictionary*, 84.
7. Clarke, *The Holy Bible: Containing the Old and New Testaments, the Text*...vol. 5, 186. Viewed at Google Books.

CHAPTER 10
THE DANGERS OF UNFORGIVENESS

1. David B. Feldman and Lee Daniel Kravatz, "Grudge Match: Can Unforgiveness Be Bad For Our Health?," Psychology Today, September 17, 2013, http://www .psychologytoday.com/blog/supersurvivors/201309/ grudge-match-can-unforgiveness-be-bad-our-health (accessed November 20, 2014).
2. Mercola.com, "New Study Shows Profound Impact of Anger on Your Health," June 17, 2010, http://articles .mercola.com/sites/articles/archive/2010/06/17/what -happens-when-you-get-angry.aspx (accessed November 20, 2014).

CHAPTER 11
HOW DO I FORGIVE?

1. John Holusha, "Students Killed by Gunman at Amish Schoolhouse," New York Times, October 2, 2006, http:// www.nytimes.com/2006/10/02/us/03amishcnd.html ?_r=0 (accessed November 20, 2014).
2. Ad Crable and Cindy Stauffer, "Nickel Mines, 5 Years Later: A Daily Walk for Amish on Path of Grief and Forgiveness," October 2, 2011, Lancaster Online, http://lancasteronline.com/news/nickel-mines-years -later-a-daily-walk-for-amish-on/article_3e48d95b -61d4-52ba-bade-7bffc61a7961.html?mode=story (accessed November 20, 2014).
3. Holusha, "Students Killed by Gunman at Amish Schoolhouse."
4. Religion News Service, "Amish Search for Healing, Forgiveness After 'The Amish 9/11,'" October 5, 2006.
5. Fox News.com, "Police: Amish School Shooter Said He Molested Kids Years Ago," October 4, 2006, http:// www.foxnews.com/story/2006/10/04/police-amish -school-shooter-said-molested-kids-years-ago/ (accessed November 20, 2014).
6. CTV, "Amish Gather to Pray at Funerals for Slain Girls," October 6, 2006; Art Carey, "Among the Amish, a Grace that Endures...," Philadelphia Inquirer, October 2, 2007, http://articles.philly.com/2007-10-02/

news/25231960_1_charles-carl-roberts-iv-nickel-mines
-rosanna-king (accessed November 20, 2014); *Amish
News*, "Amish School Shooting 2006," October 2007.

7. Damien McElroy, "Amish Killer's Widow Thanks Families of Victims for Forgiveness," October 16, 2006, http://www.telegraph.co.uk/news/worldnews/1531570/ Amish-killers-widow-thanks-families-of-victims-for -forgiveness.html (accessed November 20, 2014).
8. NPR, "The Amish Culture of Forgiveness," October 9, 2006, http://www.npr.org/templates/story/story.php ?storyId=6225726 (accessed November 20, 2014).
9. Ibid.
10. Ibid.
11. Joseph Shapiro, "Amish Forgive School Shooter, Struggle with Grief," October 2, 2007, NPR, http:// www.npr.org/templates/story/story.php?storyId =14900930 (accessed November 20, 2014).

Chapter 12
Lessons to Learn

1. Matthew Henry, *Matthew Henry's Concise Commentary on the Whole Bible* (Nashville: Thomas Nelson, 1997).
2. MADD.org, "Drunk Driving Statistics."
3. Aubrey D.N.J de Grey, "Life Span Extension Research and Publish Debate: Societal Considerations," www .sens.org/files/pdf/ENHANCE-PP.pdf (accessed November 20, 2014).
4. Kathi Pelton, "Servants of the Most High God, Come Out!", ElijahList.com, February 1, 2012, www.elijahlist .com/words/display_word.html?ID=10687 (accessed December 1, 2014).

CONTACT

www.craigstone.org

706-372-7757

EMPOWERED
TO RADICALLY CHANGE
YOUR WORLD